THE MESSIANIC ANSWER BOOK

Jewish Answers
to Jewish Questions
about The Jewish Messiah

SAM NADLER

A Note to the Reader

As you read through this book you may notice in places two varying scripture references—

ex: *(Psalm 57:2[3])*

—the first refers to the English text, the second to the Hebrew text.

*S*halom *fellow seekers,*

I hope in finding answers to your questions you will come to know Messiah, who is the very Truth of God for you now and forever. May many more of our people come to know forgiveness and joy because of what you now read.

Sam Nadler

Sam Nadler
President,
Word of Messiah Ministries

An Introduction of Sorts:
A Story of Questions and Faith

Growing up in a loving Jewish home, religion was always a mystery to me. "Jewish" was who we were, not merely what we practiced or believed. I couldn't quite understand God, though. I had many questions about the Holocaust, birth defects, unsolved crimes and other seeming contradictions to the idea of a God-ordered universe. There didn't *seem* to be any objective information for me to consider. So after my Orthodox Bar Mitzvah, (a confirmation ceremony, with chopped liver and a chorus of "Mazel Tov") I felt disinclined toward further religious involvement.

Following my stint in Viet Nam, I lived in various scenic locales of California, the "promised land" of broken promises for my generation. It was there that I ran into Jewish people who believed in "Jesus." I felt sorry for them. I thought perhaps while growing up their mothers had dressed them wrong or something, for if there's one thing any Jew should know, it's "Jews don't believe in Jesus!"

However, after looking into it for myself I got the uncomfortable feeling that there was more objective information on the matter than I had supposed. In fact, when I first read Isaiah 53 (see pages 116-118) I was shocked! I figured that those 'sneaky Christians' had stuck a portion of *their* New Testament into '*my side* of the Bible.' Nothing was supposed to be *that* clear!

After several months of further investigation I became convinced of two things.

4

First, there *is* such a thing as spiritual evil—until that time I had figured there was no objective right and wrong. It was then I realized that Eastern religion, meditation, and drugs were opening me up spiritually—but to the wrong spirit! I saw a spiritual battle for my soul, which I was losing. The second thing was, I became convinced by God and the Scriptures that Yeshua is the Messiah of Israel, and I that I needed a Savior. I needed Jesus (Yeshua's name in English).

Though I didn't know all the right words to say, I asked Yeshua to save me. And He did. When I prayed that simple prayer, I was cleansed from my sins, forgiven, and I experienced a peace that I had never known before—a peace that passes all understanding.

The Lord was gracious to me, an ordinary sinner, and I was assured that He Himself is the Answer for my life, and the lives of all my people.

To this day I still have questions, but many of my initial objections were answered by the fact of who Yeshua is *according to the Scriptures*.

In the back of this book are additional stories of faith by Jewish people—a Holocaust survivor, a professional musician, a housewife and mother, a businessman, and others—who have found 'The Messianic Answer' in Messiah Yeshua.

Some of the questions included in this publication may be your questions as well. In which case enjoy yourself, and come up with a few more for me to work through with you. In any case, here are some of the most often asked questions from our people regarding faith in Yeshua as the Messiah.

Sam Nadler

TABLE OF CONTENTS

CHAPTER 1

How Can A Jew
Believe In Jesus
And Still Be Jewish?

It depends on who Yeshua* is! The New Covenant presents Him as the *Jewish* Messiah. (John 1:41, 45, 49, etc.) If He's not the Jewish Messiah then no one should believe in Him, because His credentials as "Savior of the World" are based on His credentials as the Messiah of Israel. If He is the true Messiah, then it is kosher that I, a Jewish person, believe in Him. And I would be a Jew *in good standing with God*; even if no one else agreed.

But let's say for argument's sake, that Yeshua is a false Messiah. Still, I must still be seen as a Jew in the eyes of rabbinical authority. Why? Because, believing in a false Messiah does not make any Jew a non-Jew. In 132 A.D./A.C.E., the rebel leader Simon Bar Kochba arose during the Jewish revolt against Rome. Rabbi Akiva (a very famous Rabbi) declared Bar Kochba to be the Messiah, although at the time Bar Kochba had none of the accepted

Yeshua is the Jewish way to say Jesus.

credentials to be the Messiah. It appeared to be merely Akiva's pragmatic attempt to unite all Jews against Rome. But no Jewish authority has ever said, "Akiva is no longer Jewish for believing in a false Messiah." If, after endorsing a false messiah, Akiva is still a 'Jew in good standing', then a Jew who believes in Yeshua as the Messiah, cannot be considered otherwise.

In a Reform synagogue on Long Island, New York, following my presentation regarding why I believed Yeshua is the Messiah, the senior Rabbi stood up and declared, "Nadler, you're no longer a Jew because of your belief in Jesus!" "Rabbi," I responded, "If the Bostoner Rebbe says I'm still a Jew, though a wayward Jew, and if the Encyclopedia Judaica declares I'm still a Jew, though a wayward one, then on what basis can you say I'm 'no longer a Jew?" "Well," the Rabbi said, "perhaps I'm wrong." "Rabbi," I quietly responded, "maybe you're wrong about more than just that?" To my astonishment, the synagogue audience of more than 100 Jewish people erupted into applause. It was apparent to all who would consider the issues objectively that a Jew who believes in Yeshua is still a Jew, whether the Rabbi approves or not.

The early believers in Yeshua in the New Covenant book of John, described him as *"the Messiah;"* *"the One spoken of in Moses and the Prophets;"* *"the King of Israel, the Son of God,"* etc. They consistently saw Yeshua in a Jewish frame of reference, as fulfillment of Jewish History and Jewish lives.

Please notice also how these believers understood *themselves*. In both Acts 21:39 and 22:3 in the New Covenant, Paul declares first to the Romans, then again to his own Jewish people, **"I am a Jew from Tarsus."** Now at this time, Paul had been a believer in Yeshua for well over twenty years. So it isn't that he's confused or that he's trying to say one thing to the Romans, and something else to the Jews. Paul doesn't say that he "*was* a Jew," or that he's "an *ex*-Jew from Tarsus," or a "*former* Jew," etc.—Paul considered himself a *present tense* Jew.

In Romans 11:1, Paul reiterates his Jewish identity when he raises the rhetorical question, **"Has God forsaken His people** (Israel)**?"** He answers, **"God forbid! For I <u>am</u> an Israelite, of the seed of Abraham, of the tribe of Benjamin."** His first "proof" that God has not forsaken Israel is himself. God chose a **"Hebrew of Hebrews"** (Phil. 3:5) that the Gentile world would never think that God would forsake **"a people He foreknew."** For if the Lord would break His promises to Israel, why should anyone else think Him trustworthy regarding the Good News of Yeshua?

Today it's the same story. Every Jewish believer maintaining his/her present tense Jewish identity testifies: *"Am Yisrael Chai b'Yeshua HaMashiach." The people of Israel live in Yeshua the Messiah!*

Many Jewish people, and many non-Jews as well, are unaware that the New Covenant does not restrict in any fashion Jewish believers from identifying and living as Jewish people. There's nothing about

Jewish life that conflicts with faith in Yeshua, or with any of the New Covenant imperatives, teaching or counsel. Rather, it builds upon and fulfills the ethical, moral and spiritual teaching and revelation of God in Tanakh (the Older Covenant). In the New Covenant we read that the Jewish believers continued attending Temple (Acts 3); kept the feasts (Acts 20:6; 16; 1 Cor.16:8; etc.); circumcised their Jewish children (Acts 16:1-3); and kept other aspects of the Torah, though not being under it's "yoke" of authority (Matt. 11:29; Acts 15:10), but for the sake of identifying with and for a testimony towards their own people (1 Cor. 9:19,20).

There's a lot of "stinking thinking" on this subject even among "Christians." A few years back, I was invited to speak on a secular radio call-in show in Miami, Florida. I received a number of "you're-no-longer-a-Jew" calls from Jewish listeners. Suddenly a call came in from a more polite gentleman: "Mister Nadler, now that you're a believer in Jesus you're no longer a Jew, for the Bible says 'that in Messiah there's neither Jew nor Greek.'"

I recognized the scripture portion and responded over the air "Oh, you mean Galatians 3:28, *'There's neither Jew nor Greek, bond nor free, male nor female; for we are all one in Messiah Jesus.'*"
"Exactly," the caller replied.
"Well," I quickly said, "then let me ask you a question, please. Are you a believer?"
"Yes, I am," he answered.
"Great! Are you married?" I asked.

"Well, yes, I'm married," he slowly answered.
I asked again, "is your wife a believer?"

"Yes, she's a... believer," he responded with a longer pause.

"Is your wife a believer and still a female?" I asked. A very long pause, ands then, "Yes she'd still a female!"

"Well," I said, pausing to catch my breath. "If you're a believer and still a male, and your wife is a believer and still a female, then I'm a believer and still a Jew. The verse in Galatians is not teaching that we lose our identities in Messiah, but that there's only one way to God for all people."

An extremely long pause, then "You mean... I'm still Jewish, too?"

"If you were born a Jew," I responded, "then you're *still* a Jew."

"Hallelujah!" he shouted over the airwaves, "they had told me I was no longer Jewish."

So, if someone says "you can't believe in Jesus and still be Jewish" they need to read what the Jewish Bible teaches: Yeshua is our Messiah and trusting in Him is the most Jewish decision you can ever make!

CHAPTER 2

IF I CAN GO DIRECTLY TO GOD WHY DO I NEED A MEDIATOR?

The apocryphal story is told of U.S. President Ronald Reagan showing Israeli Prime Minister Menachem Begin his phone service in Washington.

"This red one is the hotline to Moscow, this "blackbox" is for nuclear war;" then with a flourish Reagan said, "but this gold phone is a direct line right to the Pope himself!"

Later in Jerusalem, Begin showed Reagan his communication devices.

"This red phone is a hotline to Egypt, this blue phone is to call out the troops," Begin paused, then pointing to an ordinary looking black phone he said, "that one's for spiritual matters."

"Oh, really," Reagan said, "and to whom does that phone reach?"

"Well," Begin smiled, "that phone goes directly to God Almighty!"

"How do you have a phone that can get to God?!" an amazed Reagan inquired.

"No big deal, really," Begin chuckled, "from anywhere else it's long distance, but from here in Jerusalem, it's a local call!"

This little story reflects what many people believe: Followers of Yeshua* need a mediator to get to God, but Jews have no need of a mediator and can go directly to God themselves. Though many of my Jewish people may think this assumption is true, the Jewish Scriptures teach otherwise.

Past Mediation for Israel

It may be a shock to someone's spiritual sensibilities, but at least from the days of Moses onward there was always a mediator for an Israelite to properly approach God to both hear the truth of God, as well as find forgiveness from Him.

Moses said, *"At that time I stood between the LORD and you to declare to you the word of the LORD"* (Deuteronomy 5:5).

אָנֹכִי עֹמֵד בֵּין־יְהוָה וּבֵינֵיכֶם
בָּעֵת הַהִוא לְהַגִּיד לָכֶם
אֶת־דְּבַר יְהוָה כִּי יְרֵאתֶם מִפְּנֵי הָאֵשׁ
וְלֹא־עֲלִיתֶם בָּהָר לֵאמֹר:

In fact, Israel did not want to go directly to God, but implored Moses:

"Go near and listen to all the Lord our God says. Then tell us whatever the Lord our God tells you. We will listen and obey."
(Deuteronomy 5:27; [5:24])

קְרַב אַתָּה וּשֲׁמָע אֵת כָּל־אֲשֶׁר יֹאמַר
יְהוָה אֱלֹהֵינוּ וְאַתְּ תְּדַבֵּר
אֵלֵינוּ אֵת כָּל־אֲשֶׁר יְדַבֵּר יְהוָה
אֱלֹהֵינוּ אֵלֶיךָ וְשָׁמַעְנוּ וְעָשִׂינוּ:

*Yeshua is the Jewish way to say Jesus.

Today God is considered by some to be so insignificant that anyone can "barge" into His presence. Yet the Scriptures make it an awesome and dangerous consideration for a sinner to stand before the living God! (see Psalm 24). God, unlike the rest of us, is holy. A sinful person can not stand in His holy presence without a God-appointed mediator.

Thus Moses was the recognized mediator of revelation from God to Israel. But that was not all. The Levitical priesthood (the *cohenim*) was ordained by God to be the official mediators for Israel's relationship with God through the Tabernacle, then the Temple in Jerusalem.

"Appoint Aaron and his sons to serve as priests [cohenim]; *anyone else who approaches the sanctuary must be put to death" (Numbers 3:10).*

וְאֶת־אַהֲרֹן וְאֶת־בָּנָיו תִּפְקֹד וְשָׁמְרוּ
אֶת־כְּהֻנָּתָם וְהַזָּר הַקָּרֵב יוּמָת:

Only the priests could sprinkle the offering before the altar, or enter the holy place, burn incense or perform any of the other religious ceremonies that were necessary to worship God and find acceptance in His presence (see Lev. 1:5; etc.) It was not merely ineffective for someone other than the priest to enter the presence of God to offer incense, but it was condemned; even for a king! (2 Chr. 26:16-23).

When an Israelite was back home on the farm and away from the Temple, it was only the continual daily morning and evening offerings that the priesthood presented *"as a regular burnt offering"* that gave any basis for Israel to have a spiritual life with God (Numbers 28:1-8). The mediation of the priesthood was necessary for Israel's spiritual existence.

Predicted Mediation for Israel

The Jewish Scriptures predicted God's provision of future mediation for Israel for both prophetic revelation and priestly ministration.

1

"The LORD your God will raise up for you a prophet like me from among your countrymen" (Deuteronomy 18:15, c.1400 BCE).

נָבִיא מִקִּרְבְּךָ מֵאַחֶיךָ כָּמֹנִי יָקִים
לְךָ יְהוָה אֱלֹהֶיךָ אֵלָיו תִּשְׁמָעוּן:

This way they would not have to *"hear the voice of the Lord"* themselves (Deut. 18:16). God would not provide revelation directly to each Israelite, but through the prophets, and ultimately through the Messiah, who would be...

"a light for the Gentiles" and *"a covenant for the people [Israel]"* (Isaiah 49:5-8).

2

"The LORD has sworn and will not change His mind: 'You [Messiah] *are a priest forever, in the order of Melchizedek'"*
(Psalm 110:4, circa 1000 BCE).

נִשְׁבַּע יְהוָה וְלֹא יִנָּחֵם אַתָּה־כֹהֵן
לְעוֹלָם עַל־דִּבְרָתִי מַלְכִּי־צֶדֶק:

Though the Levitical priesthood existed since

Moses, God promised a new priesthood, originating with Messiah. God would not leave his people without priestly mediation, for His desire is that we would have a proper way to draw near to Him.

3

"He will divide the spoils with the strong, because He [Messiah] poured out Himself unto death, and was numbered with the transgressors; for He bore the sin of many, and made intercession for the transgressors." (Isaiah 53:12, c. 700 BCE; full text of Isaiah 53 in Hebrew & English on page 116).

God would provide perfect intercession for all transgressors. Messiah would be the perfect sacrifice for sins, *"He bore the sin of many."* Therefore as our Mediator He would be able to provide perfect intercession for all who trust in God through Him.

Provided Mediation for Israel

With both the past and predicted mediation taught in the Jewish Scriptures, it should come as no surprise that God has fulfilled His Word, Messiah has come! He taught His followers: *"I am the way and the truth and the life; no one comes to the Father but by Me!"* (John 14:6). He was declaring what was to be expected from the true Messiah, our Mediator.

The New Covenant, in accordance with the principles of the rest of the Jewish Scriptures, states: *"For it is declared: 'You are a priest forever, in the order of Melchizedek'...because Jesus lives forever, He has a permanent priesthood. Therefore He is able to save completely those who draw near to God through Him, because He always lives to make intercession for them"* (Hebrews 7:17,24,25).

Here is the fulfillment of the mediation the God of Israel promised and was spoken of by Moses, David and Isaiah.

Right now, you can find forgiveness right where you are, through the Messiah of Israel who is ready to intercede for you, allowing you to *"draw near to God through Him."*

CHAPTER 3

DOESN'T KEEPING THE LAW KEEP ME RIGHT WITH GOD?

THE PREMISE OF THE LAW

There is a common misconception about *why* the Law, or Torah*, was given. That misconception is, that by keeping the Law the Jewish people merit righteousness before God. In other words, "We Jews don't need salvation through your Messiah Jesus because we're made holy by keeping the Law. After all, aren't the Jews God's chosen people? Haven't we been set above the other people of the world by God?" Close, but no cigar. Though this is a popular thought, it is without scriptural basis.

The Law of Moses is actually a *conditional* covenant, or agreement. Notice what God stated when the Law was given:

* Torah, or Pentateuch, is the first five books of Moses: Genesis, Exodus, Leviticus, Numbers, and Deuteronomy. "Torah" literally means "to point things out," instruction or teaching, but the commonly accepted definition is "Law."

*"Now therefore if you will obey my voice
indeed, and keep my covenant, then you will
be a special treasure to Me above all the
people; for all the earth is mine"*
(Exodus 19:5).

וְעַתָּה אִם־שָׁמוֹעַ תִּשְׁמְעוּ בְּקֹלִי וּשְׁמַרְתֶּם
אֶת־בְּרִיתִי וִהְיִיתֶם לִי סְגֻלָּה
מִכָּל־הָעַמִּים כִּי־לִי כָּל־הָאָרֶץ:

Notice the *underlined* words in the sentence. We
read the same idea in the reiteration of the Law.

*"And it shall come to pass, if you will listen
diligently to the voice of the Lord your God, to
observe and do all His commandments which
I command you this day, then the Lord your
God will set you high above all the nations of
the earth. And all these blessings shall come
on you, and overtake you, if you shall heed
the voice of the Lord your God"*
(Deut. 28:1,2).

וְהָיָה אִם־שָׁמוֹעַ תִּשְׁמַע בְּקוֹל יְהוָה אֱלֹהֶיךָ
לִשְׁמֹר לַעֲשׂוֹת אֶת־כָּל־מִצְוֹתָיו אֲשֶׁר אָנֹכִי מְצַוְּךָ
הַיּוֹם וּנְתָנְךָ יְהוָה אֱלֹהֶיךָ עֶלְיוֹן עַל כָּל־גּוֹיֵי הָאָרֶץ:
וּבָאוּ עָלֶיךָ כָּל־הַבְּרָכוֹת הָאֵלֶּה וְהִשִּׂיגֻךָ
כִּי תִשְׁמַע בְּקוֹל יְהוָה אֱלֹהֶיךָ:

Then follows twelve verses of blessings. Once
more the words *"if"* and *"then"* are *italicized.*
These words describe a conditional covenant or
agreement. The phrase "conditional covenant"
infers that the benefits are only received when the
conditions are met.

Suppose I said to my son, *"if* you clean your
room, *then* I will give you a dollar." If he didn't

clean his room, he could not expect to receive the payment. If he partially cleaned his room, would I be bound to pay him? If I wrote up the agreement the way that God wrote the Torah, I would owe him nothing. For you see, in the above Deuteronomy portion another word is highlighted, *"all."* God's obligation to reward His people depends on them first obeying **all** (כָּל, kol) His commandments. There are 613 laws in the Jewish Scriptures. Any expectation for rightful blessing under the Law is dependent upon our perfect obedience to the Law.

As if this is not clear enough, the Deuteronomy portion restates the same idea in the negative:

> ***"But it shall come to pass that if you will
> not heed the voice of the Lord your God,
> to observe to do all His commandments and
> His statutes which I command you today,
> then all these curses shall come upon you
> and overtake you"***
> *(Deut. 28:15).*

וְהָיָה אִם־לֹא תִשְׁמַע בְּקוֹל יְהוָה
אֱלֹהֶיךָ לִשְׁמֹר לַעֲשׂוֹת אֶת־כָּל־מִצְוֹתָיו
וְחֻקֹּתָיו אֲשֶׁר אָנֹכִי מְצַוְּךָ הַיּוֹם וּבָאוּ
עָלֶיךָ כָּל־הַקְּלָלוֹת הָאֵלֶּה וְהִשִּׂיגוּךָ:

Thereafter follows 53 verses of curses.

So what happens if there is imperfect obedience, if even one commandment is disobeyed? If you don't do "all" God legislated, then all the curses will come upon you. To those of us that see sincere effort as "good enough," this can seem shocking and unfair: "How does God expect anyone to get blessed with that impossible standard? Doesn't He want to bless His people?" This brings us to the purpose of the Law.

The Purpose of the Law

The purpose of Torah is to demonstrate how holy God is and our desperate need for His mercy. Its purpose was never to reveal how good we are or how deserving we are of God's blessing.

God had made an *un*conditional covenant with Abraham (Genesis 12:1-3 etc.). On the basis of the Abrahamic Covenant the Jewish people's existence and survival (and land) is guaranteed. But if we think such great promises demonstrate our worthiness rather than God's graciousness, God provided the Torah to show what we're *really* like (Deu. 9:6).

In the Law itself there are provisions for our moral failures (sins). That's why there's so much material on the sacrifices for sin (Leviticus chapters 1-7, etc.) and the need for atonement, as in Yom Kippur, the Day of Atonement. A cursory yet objective reading of the Scriptures makes it plain; the Law reveals our sinfulness not our righteousness. The Law is like a perfect mirror that can only reveal our flaws, but can do nothing to improve them.

The Promise beyond the Law

Not only can we not adequately keep the Law, but the Law cannot keep us as a people either. We are kept as a people (and even blessed) by God's mercy and gracious promises. When Israel's sin of the Golden Calf deserved God's utter destruction (Ex. 32:10), Moses didn't plead for their welfare on the basis of the Law he had just delivered, but on the basis of the *Abrahamic Covenant (Ex. 32:13).

* The Abrahamic Covenant promised to sustain a people, but was not the means to save an individual. This is why even Abraham had to repent and make sacrifice (Genesis 13:4, 18), and have faith (Genesis 15:6). This is also why he was glad to hope in Messiah (John 8:56), Who would be God's ultimate sacrifice for sin and salvation.

The Law allowed God the prerogative to judge His people by His objective, holy, legal standard. God wants His people to recognize His holiness, the evil of their sins, and absolute graciousness of His promises.

The Law in all of its holy demands upon Israel—*"You shall be Holy even as the Lord your God is holy" (Lev. 19:2)*—demonstrated Israel's constant need for mercy. This would prepare God's people for the coming of His ultimate demonstration of mercy, Messiah. God's Messiah would provide final atonement for sins through His own sacrifice:

"He was bruised for our iniquity... The Lord laid on Him the iniquity of us all... He was cut off out of the land of the living, for the transgressions of my people, to whom the judgment was due... He bore the sin of many"
(Isaiah 53:5,6,8,12).
(See full text of Isaiah 53 on page 107).

As we read the actual Scriptures, as opposed to the rabbinical traditions concerning the Law, we face a holy and yet loving God. Before Him we all fall morally short. But we also see One who has mercifully provided the promise of forgiveness and life to all who will trust in His Word.

Individually as Jews, or corporately as Israel, it is the gracious promise of God that is our hope. This promise is fulfilled in Yeshua HaMashiach*, even as the New Covenant proclaims:

"...Him of whom Moses in the Law and the Prophets did write" (John 1:45).

*The Jewish way to say 'Jesus the Messiah'.

CHAPTER 4

You Mean, The Jewish Scriptures Teach About Hell?

When we read the Scriptures we discover that they don't attempt to prove God exists, rather, God is presented as a reality. Just as one never has to prove the reality of parents to a child, the child's own existence proves there must also be biological parents. So also, one need not prove the reality of the Creator to the creature.

The Fact of Hell

Hell is likewise presented. The absolute holiness and justice of God requires it. If a person can get a life sentence without possibility of parole for evil perpetrated against a mere man, then why should it seem so strange for one to get an eternal life sentence for evil perpetrated against the Eternal God?

The Psalmist writes,

> *"The wicked will return to Sheol, even all the nations who forget God"* *(Psalm 9:17).*

"Let death come deceitfully upon them; let them go down alive to Sheol, for evil is in their dwelling, in their midst" (Psalm 55:15).

The psalmist uses the word *Sheol*, the common word for Hell. However, since all people die, the writer is not referring merely to death or 'the grave'—which would be no great punishment for the wicked—but to the eternal punishment of Sheol/Hell.

The Prophet Isaiah writes, *"Nevertheless, you will be thrust down to Sheol, to the recesses of the pit. Those who see you will gaze at you, they will ponder over you saying, 'Is this the man who made the world tremble, who shook kingdoms..." (Isaiah 14:15,16).* The Prophet reveals that there is consciousness, recognition and communication for those in Sheol/Hell.

The Prophet Daniel writes, *"And many of those that sleep in the dust of the ground will awake, these to everlasting life, but the others to disgrace and everlasting contempt" (Dan. 12:2).* Daniel reveals that the final judgment of Sheol/Hell that follows death, is *"everlasting"* (*"olam"* which also means heaven, or everlasting life), and is *disgrace*ful and *contempt*ible (literally, an abhorrence).

The New Covenant is consistent with the Older Covenant regarding these same truths about Hell/Sheol: *(Matthew 25:41, "eternal fire"; v.46 "eternal punishment"; Mark 9:43-48 "into Hell, into the unquenchable fire"; 2 Thessalonians 1:9 "pay the penalty of eternal destruction"; Hebrews*

*9:27, **"it is appointed for man to die once and after this comes judgment"; Rev. 14:11 "...the smoke of their torment goes up forever and ever, and they have no rest day or night..."***).

It's not that the Bible attempts to frighten anyone into following God, but it does reveal the facts of the hereafter. Actually, the amount of space the Scriptures spend on Hell is comparatively very little. The Bible generally reveals Great News about God, Messiah, love, Heaven, forgiveness, etc.

The Fairness of Hell

What seems most difficult to some is what appears to be the inherent unfairness of Hell. "After all," some might think, "why would a good person have to be punished alongside of 'a Hitler' just because he didn't follow God's way? Isn't that unfair?"

First, let's understand that no one deserves Heaven. This is God's special place and no one who sins deserves to be there (see Psalm 15:1). God's standards for Heaven are high: to be with Him, you must be like Him, **"Be holy as the LORD your God is holy"** *(Leviticus 19:2).*

Therefore whoever goes to Heaven *doesn't earn it*—entrance to Heaven is *not* based on fairness. Whoever goes to Heaven has been received on the basis of God's sovereign, gracious love. On the other hand, since we all have sinned (see Ps. 14:3; Isa. 53:6; etc.) we all deserve Hell. We earned it. How to avoid Hell is brought up later in this article.

The Scripture teaches that each one gets the punishment in Hell they individually deserve. There are differing degrees of punishment in Hell, determined completely on what you deserve, and similarly, there are differing degrees of reward in Heaven.

The Degrees of Punishment in Hell

1. Judged according to their Deeds:
   "…The dead, the great and the small,
   were standing before the throne…
   And the dead were judged…
   according to their deeds"
   (Rev. 20:12).

This portion teaches that if Bill and Joel were doomed to judgment, and during their lifetimes Bill stole ten cars, but Joel only stole one car (or told ten lies to one lie, etc.), Bill's punishment would be ten times greater than Joel's punishment because his evil deeds were ten times worse. That's fair.

2. Judged according to their Knowledge:
   "And the servant that knew his master's will and
   did not get ready or act in accord with that will,
   shall receive much punishment. But the one that
   did not know it, and committed deeds worthy of
   punishment, will receive little punishment.
   To whom much is given, much will be required"
   (Luke 12:47,48).

Now, let's say Bill and Joel were both doomed to hell, and during their lifetime each of them stole ten cars. This portion teaches that if Bill learned that's it's wrong to steal and stole anyway, but Joel did not learn this truth, Bill's punishment would be greater than Joel's, because Bill knew better. He will be held more accountable for the knowledge he

27

received. Joel still gets punished, for he still did deeds worthy of punishment, but to a lesser degree. That, too, is fair.

3. Judged according to their "Rank":
"Not many of you should presume to be teachers, my brothers, because you know that we who teach will be judged more strictly"
(James 3:1).

This portion teaches that if Bill and Joel were both doomed to hell, and both stole ten cars, but Bill was the teacher (or leader, Rabbi, Priest, Pastor, President, etc.) his punishment would be greater than Joel's since Bill's position demanded a higher level of responsibility. Rank may, or may not, have its privileges, but it certainly has greater accountability before God. Again, this is fair.

The Scriptures teach that Hell is very fair. Tragically, in Hell people finally get what they justly deserve.

The Fleeing from Hell
"The rich man also died and was buried. In Hell, where he was in torment... he called... 'I have five brothers...warn them, so they will not also come to this place of torment'"
(Luke 16:23-27).

Many times people might foolishly say "I want to be with my buddies in Hell," or "I want to be with my brother and father in Hell." But, do you know what their buddies and family want? They want to warn you and everybody else to do whatever it takes to avoid Hell!

God wants you to avoid Hell and go to Heaven. He cannot overlook sin, but He does love you.

That's why He sent the Messiah, Yeshua.

Yeshua died as atonement for sins, just as the Jewish prophets predicted (*see Isaiah 53 on page 116*). All who will trust in God's provision for forgiveness have new life and heaven as a gift of God.

God desperately wants you in Heaven. But you must choose to receive God's free gift of eternal life in Yeshua in order to escape Hell and be in Heaven forever. He will not save you against your will. That's only fair.

CHAPTER 5

Why Do We Need a Sacrifice to Atone for Sins?

Often, modern, 'educated' people tend to object to the idea of sin and sacrifice: "I don't need a sacrifice! I can just repent." "I'm basically a good person." "I'm good enough. Besides, sin isn't all that important anyway." To many folks, those concerned with sin and sacrifice (like followers of Messiah Yeshua) seem to be either neurotically obsessed with sin, or naively barbaric for extolling sacrifice- maybe even both!

The Issue of Sin Minimized

For most people "sin and sacrifice" are just not very relevant issues. "Sin" for the most part is viewed as a "moral lapse in judgment" and is "atoned" for with something between a sincere apology and a life sentence. The basic consideration is that "people are generally good," with a few obvious exceptions.

I remember handing out some Good News literature several years ago in New York City a few weeks after *Yom Kippur* (the Day of Atonement). I saw one of New York's finest, and since his Police ID revealed he was from "my side of the family", I offered him a brochure.

When he saw that the title spoke of the need for atonement and forgiveness, he said, "Forget it; I don't need that. The people I arrest need *that* message."

"Really," I said, "and where were you on Yom Kippur?"

"In the synagogue," he shot back, "where I was supposed to be!"

"And what did you do in the synagogue?" I asked. "Why I was…" and his voice trailed off as his fist began automatically beating his chest, as all orthodox Jews are trained to do as they repent of sins on that day.

His voice changed and he said, "Okay, I'll read one of your pamphlets." As he thought of Yom Kippur, he remembered that on the Day of Atonement, everyone must acknowledge that they have sinned.

As Jewish people, we know that at least once a year we are reminded by the Torah not to be self-righteous (Leviticus 23:29). In *The Prophets* and *The Writings* (Psalms, Proverbs, etc.), the Scriptures are perfectly clear as well regarding the sinful nature of people:

> ***"All we, like sheep, have gone astray;***
> ***each one has turned to his own way"***
> *(Isaiah 53:6; see full text of Isaiah 53 on page 116).*

"All of us are as an unclean thing, and all our righteousnesses as filthy rags" (Isaiah 64:6).

וַנְּהִי כַטָּמֵא כֻּלָּנוּ וּכְבֶגֶד עִדִּים כָּל־צִדְקֹתֵינוּ

"The heart is deceitful above all things, and desperately wicked, who can know it"
(Jeremiah 17:9).

עָקֹב הַלֵּב מִכֹּל וְאָנֻשׁ הוּא מִי יֵדָעֶנּוּ׃

"There is none that does good, no, not one"
(Psalm 14:3).

אֵין עֹשֵׂה־טוֹב אֵין גַּם אֶחָד׃

"In Your sight no man can be justified"
(Psalm 143:2).

כִּי לֹא־יִצְדַּק לְפָנֶיךָ כָל־חָי

God calls *sin* (rebellion and disobedience to God) *wicked* and deserving of judgment. For a person to call sin 'unimportant' doesn't make it any less wicked. Just as changing the label on a bottle of rat poison to read "fruit juice" doesn't make the contents any less deadly. In fact, now it becomes even more dangerous, since someone may think that taking a drink could actually be nutritious!

If this seems like an overstatement, understand that the Scriptures reveal just how disastrous sin is:
The Prophet Ezekiel said,

"The soul that sins, it shall die!" (Ezekiel 18:3).

הַנֶּפֶשׁ הַחֹטֵאת הִיא תָמוּת

This is the eternal judgment that is also spoken of by Daniel the Prophet. There is a time of resurrection when eternal judgment will be dispensed:

"Those who sleep in the dust of the earth
will awake, some to everlasting life
and some to everlasting contempt" (Daniel 12:2).

וְרַבִּים מִיְשֵׁנֵי אַדְמַת־עָפָר יָקִיצוּ אֵלֶּה
לְחַיֵּי עוֹלָם וְאֵלֶּה לַחֲרָפוֹת לְדִרְאוֹן עוֹלָם:

Isaiah reveals that though people think they pray and are heard by God, their sins actually break that 'prayer connection':

"It's not that God is unable to hear you or help you, but your sins have made a separation between God and you, so that He will not hear you" *(Isaiah 59:1,2).*

הֵן לֹא־קָצְרָה יַד־יְהוָה מֵהוֹשִׁיעַ וְלֹא־כָבְדָה
אָזְנוֹ מִשְּׁמוֹעַ: כִּי אִם־עֲוֺנֹתֵיכֶם הָיוּ מַבְדִּלִים בֵּינֵכֶם
לְבֵין אֱלֹהֵיכֶם וְחַטֹּאותֵיכֶם הִסְתִּירוּ
פָנִים מִכֶּם מִשְּׁמוֹעַ:

God's way of Atonement

God's way of forgiving sins is as misunderstood as the problem of sin. People often discuss whether the Temple, which was a place of sacrifices, will ever be rebuilt in Jerusalem. The problem with rebuilding the Temple is not a Muslim Mosque atop the Temple Mount, but 2000 years of traditional rabbinical teaching. Tradition has erroneously taught our people that we do not need *blood atonement* for sins. But, the Scriptures state that blood sacrifice *alone* can atone for sins:

"The life of the flesh is in the blood; and I have given it to you upon the altar to make atonement for your souls; for it is the blood that makes atonement for the soul" *(Lev. 17:11).*

כִּי נֶפֶשׁ הַבָּשָׂר בַּדָּם הוּא וַאֲנִי נְתַתִּיו
לָכֶם עַל־הַמִּזְבֵּחַ לְכַפֵּר עַל־נַפְשֹׁתֵיכֶם
כִּי־הַדָּם הוּא בַּנֶּפֶשׁ יְכַפֵּר:

In fact, Yom Kippur is only a Day of Atonement if atonement is made God's way: *by the blood sacrifice* (see Leviticus 16). Merely acknowledging your sins and even repenting of them, is no more effective than for someone, in an attempt to dismiss a murder charge, to 'apologize' to the offended party! Sin is that horrific to God, and He is the offended party.

Messiah is God's final Sacrifice for Atonement

All the sacrifices of Scripture were to illustrate the final, perfect sacrifice that God himself would provide in the Messiah.

"Surely He has borne our griefs and carried our sorrows; yet we esteemed Him stricken and afflicted by God. But he was wounded for our transgressions, he was bruised for our iniquities…the lord has laid on Him the iniquity of us all…He was cut off from the land of the living for the transgression of my people was He stricken…He shall make His soul an offering for sin…My righteous Servant shall justify the many, for He shall bear their iniquities…He bore the sin of many and made intercession for the transgressors" (Isaiah 53:3-12; the full text of Isaiah 53 is on page 116).

Here is pictured for us God's provision for our sins through the Messiah's atonement.

The prophet begins the chapter by asking, *"Who has believed our report?"* (Isaiah 53:1). That's still the question today: Who will believe God, His view of sin, and His way of forgiveness?

The New Covenant provides what the Hebrew Scriptures predicted: ***"God demonstrates His own love toward us, in that while we were yet sinners, Messiah died for us"*** *(Romans 5:8).*

All who trust in Messiah Yeshua* for their atonement receive forgiveness for their sins, and best of all, an eternal relationship with God!

Yeshua is the Jewish way to say Jesus.

CHAPTER 6

HOW CAN A MAN BECOME GOD?

Sometimes humor can best illustrate a biblical *mis*understanding.

An Irish man was talking with his Jewish friend:

"Saul, did you hear the great news? My son Patty has become a priest!"

"So what's the big deal about that, John?" Saul asked.

"It's a very big deal, Saul. As a priest he can one day become a bishop!" John responded.

"So what's the big deal about that?" Saul again asked.

"Saul, as a bishop, Patty can one day become a cardinal. Imagine, my son, the Cardinal!" John was getting excited now.

"Nu," Saul blasted, "but what's the big deal about that, John?"

John sputtered out, "Saul, my friend, as Cardinal, Patty could be...Oh, be still my heart...he could become Pope!"

And Saul again asked, "So nu, what's the big deal about that, John?"

Now impatient, John demanded, "So what do you expect, for him to become God?!!"
Almost triumphantly, Saul said, "and why not, one of *our* boys made it!"

The biblical *mis*understanding is this: that Yeshua*, a man, became God. This is *not* the message of the Scriptures. The Scriptures are quite clear on this point: no man can become God! But on the other hand, *"nothing is impossible for God!"* (Genesis 18:14; Luke 1:37). What the Jewish Scriptures prophesied and the New Covenant declares is that in Yeshua, God (Adonai) became a man—He came in the flesh. Three questions normally raised on this issue help us consider it more fully.

Can God come 'in the flesh'?

To find this answer let's visit Abraham in Genesis 18. In Genesis 18:1 the text states that…*"The LORD appeared to Abraham by the Oaks of Mamre."*

וַיֵּרָא אֵלָיו יְהוָה בְּאֵלֹנֵי מַמְרֵא

In the next verse it states that *"as he lifted his eyes, three men stood by him."* Abraham and Sarah then prepared food for these "guests" (see 18:3-8). Was it merely a vision? Impossible, for not only do you *not* prepare food for a vision, but visions don't eat! And these 'men' did (*"and they ate"*, 18:8).

Now, two of these three 'men' are later identified as angels (compare Genesis 18:22 and 19:1). But the third One who ate (v.8), spoke (v.10), and walked with Abraham (v.16, 22) is identified as the LORD Himself. In Genesis 18:13, the text states:

*Yeshua is the Jewish way to say Jesus.

"And the LORD said to Abraham...."

וַיֹּאמֶר יְהוָה אֶל־אַבְרָהָם

The word translated **LORD** throughout this portion is called the *Tetragrammaton*—the four Hebrew letters that make up the sacred Name of God. These are יהוה, *yood, hey, vav, hey* (pronounced by some as 'Yahweh', or even 'Jehovah').

Do the Jewish Scriptures teach that God came in the flesh? Clearly the answer is yes!

Bᴜᴛ, Bɪʙʟɪᴄᴀʟʟʏ, ᴡᴀs Mᴇssɪᴀʜ ᴇxᴘᴇᴄᴛᴇᴅ ᴛᴏ ʙᴇ 'Gᴏᴅ Iɴᴄᴀʀɴᴀᴛᴇ'?

The Prophets, especially Isaiah and Micah, most directly answer this.

ISAiAʜ ᴡʀᴏᴛᴇ:

"For a child shall be born to us and a son shall be given; and the government shall be upon His shoulder; and His name shall be called: Wonderful Counselor, Mighty God, Everlasting Father, Prince of Peace"
(Isaiah 9:6 [v.5]).

כִּי־יֶלֶד יֻלַּד־לָנוּ בֵּן נִתַּן־לָנוּ
וַתְּהִי הַמִּשְׂרָה עַל־שִׁכְמוֹ וַיִּקְרָא שְׁמוֹ
פֶּלֶא יוֹעֵץ אֵל גִּבּוֹר אֲבִיעַד שַׂר־שָׁלוֹם:

This portion is traditionally recognized as referring to Messiah: **"'I have yet to raise up the Messiah,' of whom it is written,** *for a child is born to us* **[Isaiah 9:5]"** (Midrash Rabbah on Deuteronomy/Debarim, p. 22).

Isaiah predicts that one coming from the *"Galilee"* (9:1) will bring *"light," "joy"* (9:2,3) and *"victorious peace"* (9:4,5) because He is the **Prince of Peace (Sar Shalom)** indeed, the **Mighty God (El Gibbor)**. This child to be born is the theme of Isaiah 7:12. Where it states He would be *"born of a virgin,"* (הָעַלְמָה הָרָה, 7:14) He is *"the root of David"* that *"Gentiles will trust in"* (11:10), as well **the remnant of Israel** (10:20-23). The truth of who this One will be is reiterated when the Scripture says that not every Jewish person will believe, but only a remnant: ***"the remnant shall return, the remnant of Jacob, to the Mighty God"*** *[El Gibbor]* (10:21).

שְׁאָר יָשׁוּב שְׁאָר יַעֲקֹב אֶל־אֵל גִּבּוֹר:

Micah

Micah the prophet not only gives further detail about Messiah's Divine Nature, but also specifically where He would be born.

"But you, Bethlehem Ephratah, little among the thousands of Judah, out of you will go forth for Me, one who will be ruler in Israel, whose goings forth have been from <u>days of eternity</u>"
(Micah 5:2 [v.1]).

וְאַתָּה בֵּית־לֶחֶם אֶפְרָתָה צָעִיר
לִהְיוֹת בְּאַלְפֵי יְהוּדָה מִמְּךָ לִי יֵצֵא
לִהְיוֹת מוֹשֵׁל בְּיִשְׂרָאֵל וּמוֹצָאֹתָיו
מִקֶּדֶם מִימֵי עוֹלָם:

Micah clearly states that Israel's Ruler would not only be "born," in Bethlehem, but his *"goings forth"* would be from **eternity** (עוֹלָם, olam). That is, He who would be born in Bethlehem *is* God, the Eternal One!

Thus the Messiah, the One to bring peace, joy

and life to all who would believe ("the remnant"), the One who would be born in Bethlehem, yet live in Galilee, this One is the LORD, the Mighty God Himself!

But, does the New Covenant proclaim Yeshua as Messiah and God?

The word *"Christ"* is a transliteration, *not* a translation, from the Greek word, *"Christos"* meaning "Anointed One." It should be translated *"Messiah"*. Thus, "Christ" is not Yeshua's last name, but His title—Messiah. Hundreds of times the New Covenant unequivocally declares Yeshua to be the Messiah. Similarly, His Deity is declared hundreds of times as well, by His title 'Lord' and His identification as *the* LORD of the Older Covenant (Tanakh, or Old Testament). Please note that when referring to Yeshua, the New Covenant repeatedly uses portions of the Tanakh that actually refer to God (see for example Mark 1:1-3, Heb. 1:8-12). The New Covenant writers were clear regarding Messiah's Divine nature:

"In the beginning was the Word, the Word was with God, the Word was God....and the Word became flesh and dwelt among us.." (John 1:1,14).

Mostly, Yeshua's Divinity was assumed, and written about in order to make an application for our lives:

"Each of you should not look merely to your own interests but also to the interests of others. Your attitude should be the same as Messiah's. Who being in very nature God, did not consider equality with God something to be grasped, but humbled

Himself, taking on the form of a servant, coming in human appearance. In that form of a man, He humbled Himself and became obedient unto death, even death by the cross" (Philippians 2:4-8).

What amazing love is demonstrated in the humility of our Messiah! The One who is the Eternal God, Adonai, came in the flesh to die for our sins, that we might have forgiveness, life, joy and peace by trusting in His atoning sacrifice for our sins.

No man can become God, but God became a man in Yeshua, the Messiah of Israel and Savior of the World. Through His incarnation, God's Life and Love is available to all who will believe!

CHAPTER 7

If the Messiah Has Already Come, Then Why Isn't There Peace?

The story goes something like this: a person considering whether Yeshua* is the Messiah, asks his Rabbi, "Could it be that Messiah has come and that Yeshua is His name?" The Rabbi walks over to the window, looks outside, shakes his head and with a sigh exclaims: "He can't be the true Messiah. There's still no peace. We know that when Messiah comes there will be peace everywhere."

Is it true that Messiah is to bring peace? And if Yeshua is the Messiah, then where's the peace?

The Promise of Peace

The desire for peace is universal among the sane nations of this world. The idea of peace means much more than merely the end of hostilities. The Hebrew word for peace, *shalom*, has in it the idea of completeness or wholeness. The Scriptures tell us that because of sin we're all incomplete. Sin

Yeshua is the Jewish way to say Jesus.

separates us from God and each other and even ourselves. The *shalom,* or peace, of God fulfills us perfectly and completely.

This is also the very desire of God, who in Aaron's blessing states:
"May the Lord give you peace" *(Numbers 6:26).*

וְיָשֵׂם לְךָ שָׁלוֹם:

The Psalmist writes:
"The Lord will bless His people with peace"
(Psalm 29:11).

יִתֵּן יְהוָה יְבָרֵךְ אֶת־עַמּוֹ בַשָּׁלוֹם:

And in the Prophets, Messiah is even called ***"Prince of Peace"*** *(Isaiah 9:6[5]).*

שַׂר־שָׁלוֹם

In fact, when Messiah reigns, peace will be His Kingdom's theme (Isaiah 2:1-4; 9:4-5,7; Zechariah 9:9,10; etc.).

But, the universal peace of Messiah is first based on each person having personal peace through a right relationship with God:
"You will keep him in perfect peace whose mind is steadfast, because he trusts in You"
(Isaiah 26:3).

יֵצֶר סָמוּךְ תִּצֹּר שָׁלוֹם שָׁלוֹם כִּי בְךָ בָּטוּחַ:

Thus when each person receives peace from God, then each one can live in, and share that peace within their family, community, country and world. This peace is like wishing you had a million dollars that you could share with a friend. Of course, if you don't have it, you don't have it to give.

The Rejection of Peace

The Scriptures prophesy that God's peace would actually be rejected when it would be offered. Isaiah the Prophet wrote that Messiah, the "Prince of Peace" (*Sar Shalom*, Isaiah 9:6[5]), would come to make peace between God and His people. Isaiah also predicted that the Messiah would be rejected by our people. When Messiah would be rejected, the peace He would bring would be rejected along with Him. Why would Israel reject her Messiah?

"He had no beauty or majesty to attract us to Him, nothing in His appearance that we should be attracted to Him" (Isaiah 53:2).

וַיַּעַל כַּיּוֹנֵק לְפָנָיו וְכַשֹּׁרֶשׁ מֵאֶרֶץ
צִיָּה לֹא־תֹאַר לוֹ וְלֹא הָדָר וְנִרְאֵהוּ
וְלֹא־מַרְאֶה וְנֶחְמְדֵהוּ:

For people attracted to externals, Messiah would be too ordinary looking. There was nothing about His appearance to command our attention. But for those who could see it, His internal character made Him "stand out":

"He was a man of sorrows and familiar with suffering. Surely, He took upon Himself our griefs and sorrows, yet we considered Him stricken by God and afflicted by Him"
(Isaiah 53:3,4).

נִבְזֶה וַחֲדַל אִישִׁים אִישׁ מַכְאֹבוֹת וִידוּעַ חֹלִי
וּכְמַסְתֵּר פָּנִים מִמֶּנּוּ נִבְזֶה וְלֹא חֲשַׁבְנֻהוּ:
אָכֵן חֳלָיֵנוּ הוּא נָשָׂא וּמַכְאֹבֵינוּ סְבָלָם וַאֲנַחְנוּ
חֲשַׁבְנֻהוּ נָגוּעַ מֻכֵּה אֱלֹהִים וּמְעֻנֶּה:

For people desirous of comfort and convenience, this One suffered too much. How could one suffer so much at the hands of religious people and the government, and not be under the judgment of God? No "decent" person would want to be associated with someone who attracted trouble the way this "Messiah" did! But Yeshua suffered for *our* sins, rather than His own:

"The Lord laid on Him the iniquity of us all"
(Isaiah 53:6).

וַיהוָה הִפְגִּיעַ בּוֹ אֵת עֲוֺן כֻּלָּנוּ:

"He was brought as a lamb to the slaughter, as a sheep before the shearers is silent, so He did not open His mouth" (Isaiah 53:7).

נִגַּשׂ וְהוּא נַעֲנֶה וְלֹא יִפְתַּח־פִּיו כַּשֶּׂה לַטֶּבַח

יוּבָל וּכְרָחֵל לִפְנֵי גֹזְזֶיהָ נֶאֱלָמָה וְלֹא יִפְתַּח פִּיו:

Yeshua was too compliant, too passive. He wasn't exactly the "John Wayne/Arnold Swartznegger" type of warrior King. Many wanted a Messiah who would come to vanquish the enemies of Israel, and thus have a forced peace. Messiah's humility was despised and rejected, for He came not to protect His own life, but to give His life as an offering for our sins:

"The Lord makes His life a guilt offering"
(Isaiah 53:10).

וַיהוָה חָפֵץ דַּכְּאוֹ הֶחֱלִי אִם־תָּשִׂים אָשָׁם נַפְשׁוֹ

Now suppose I came to your house with a beautiful cake (my father always taught me not to visit empty handed), but as soon as you saw me you slammed the door in my face! Would you expect to get the cake? Of course not! Reject me, and you reject all that I bring with me. So, why isn't there peace? Reject the Prince of Peace and you reject the very peace that He brings.

THE PROVISION OF PEACE

The New Covenant Scriptures fulfill the promise of Isaiah 26:3 (see pg. 43). All who will trust in Messiah Yeshua and the atonement that He made for sins, will receive:

PEACE WITH GOD...

"Therefore, since we're made right with God by faith, we have peace with God through Yeshua HaMashiach Adoneinu
[Yeshua the Messiah our Lord]" (Romans 5:1).

PEACE OF MIND AND HEART...

"The peace of God, which is beyond all understanding, will guard your hearts and minds in Messiah Yeshua" (Philippians 4:7).

PEACE WITH ONE ANOTHER...

"Messiah is our peace,
who has made the two (Jews and Gentiles) one...
one new person, thus making peace"
(Ephesians 2:14-15).

The Scriptures also teach that one day our people, Israel, will acknowledge Yeshua as the Messiah and receive His salvation and peace:

"The stone which the builders rejected shall become the chief cornerstone!" (Psalms 118:22).

אֶבֶן מָאֲסוּ הַבּוֹנִים הָיְתָה לְרֹאשׁ פִּנָּה:

In light of that event we are commanded to *"Pray for the peace of Jerusalem" (Psalm 122:6).*

שַׁאֲלוּ שְׁלוֹם יְרוּשָׁלָם

In that day, peace will be worldwide, for the Prince of Peace will reign over the nations, over Israel and over each person's heart, even as the Scriptures promised.

An illustration of that coming day was seen in Israel a few years ago. An Israeli soldier, a fervent believer in Yeshua, was on patrol one night in Gaza. After coming upon a suspiciously parked van, the others in his squad had him, the "believer", investigate, which in that part of the world can be quite dangerous. The Israeli soldier cautiously approached the scene, and came upon the driver. After interrogating him, he discovered that the driver was a Palestinian pastor, a believer in Yeshua, visiting some of his congregants. As the other soldiers looked on from a safe distance, to their amazement, here was an Israeli Jew and a Palestinian laughing and rejoicing in fellowship in the Gaza moonlight. Needless to say, the other Israelis had many questions to ask their fellow soldier when he returned to the squad!

Yeshua is Israel's, and the world's, only hope for peace. But until that coming day, right now each one of us can individually have peace with God, within our own hearts and with one another by trusting in Israel's Messiah, Yeshua.

"Trusting in the Lord" begins by recognizing that neither the world's peace plans nor our own strategies for personal peace have worked. Then trusting in Messiah Yeshua, as He is God's way to have peace in your life and "peace on earth, goodwill for all people."

CHAPTER 8

Do You Really Expect Me to Believe in Three Gods?

Of course not!
New Covenant faith is Jewish and teaches Monotheism.

One of the great misconceptions about the faith of New Covenant believers is that "they believe in three gods." However, the clear teachings in the New Covenant prove otherwise :

> *"And Jesus answered him and said 'The first of all the commandments is: Hear O Israel, the Lord our God is one Lord'"* (Mark 12:29; see also 1 Cor. 8:4; James 2:19, etc.).

Thus, New Covenant faith is *biblically* Jewish. However, because of the ignorance of scriptural teaching on the *"tri-unity" of God, there is confusion on the subject.

---

*The word "trinity" is a contraction of "tri-unity."

The Testimony of The Jewish Scriptures

As we look into Jewish Scriptures we see the mystery nature of God presented:

"Hear O Israel, the Lord our God is one Lord"
(Deuteronomy 6:4).

שְׁמַע יִשְׂרָאֵל יְהוָה אֱלֹהֵינוּ יְהוָה אֶחָד:

As one Jewish man commented to me, "God is mentioned three times right there in Deuteronomy 6:4, the verse that speaks of His oneness!" "But," one might object, "it says *one* in the verse." True, but the word "one" (אֶחָד, *echad,* in the original Hebrew), can be a *one* of "complex unity." For example, when God established the marriage relationship, the Scripture states:

"For this cause a man shall leave his father and mother and cleave to his wife; and the two shall be <u>one</u> flesh" *(Gen. 2:24).*

עַל־כֵּן יַעֲזָב־אִישׁ אֶת־אָבִיו וְאֶת־אִמּוֹ
וְדָבַק בְּאִשְׁתּוֹ וְהָיוּ לְבָשָׂר אֶחָד:

Here we see that "one" is used when clearly there is not one in the absolute sense, but as a complex unity. In another text of scripture this complex unity is explained further:

"And they came to the brook of Eshcol and cut down from there a branch with one cluster of grapes" (Numbers 13:23).

וְאֶשְׁכּוֹל עֲנָבִים אֶחָד

Here again *one* is used to refer to a cluster, which is a complex unity.

There is another word for **one** in Hebrew, יָחִיד, **yachid**. *Yachid* is used in Gen. 22:2 when God is speaking to Abraham about Isaac.

> *"Take now your son, your <u>only</u> son."*
>
> קַח־נָא אֶת־בִּנְךָ אֶת־יְחִידְךָ

Though Abraham had another son, Ishmael, God refers to Isaac as a one-of-a-kind son, the son of the covenant. This word is used for an absolute, singular, one, and **never used for God in the Bible!**

This complex nature of God is *assumed* in the Scripture, rather than *explained*. That's why a portion like the following one in Genesis can only make sense in light of this assumption:

> *"**The Lord** (Who was on the earth speaking with Abraham) **rained upon Sodom brimstone and fire** <u>**from the Lord out of heaven**</u>" (Gen. 19:24).*
>
> וַיהוָה הִמְטִיר עַל־סְדֹם וְעַל־עֲמֹרָה
> גָּפְרִית וָאֵשׁ מֵאֵת יְהוָה מִן־הַשָּׁמָיִם:

In the creation account in Genesis 1:26 where God created man, we are brought into the counsels of God's own heart:

> *"And God said, 'Let us make man in <u>our</u> image, according to <u>our</u> likeness" (Gen. 1:26).*
>
> וַיֹּאמֶר אֱלֹהִים נַעֲשֶׂה אָדָם בְּצַלְמֵנוּ כִּדְמוּתֵנוּ

Please notice the plural possessive pronoun, **'our'**. By using this word *'Our'*, God reveals His own complex nature. The Scripture goes on to say,

> *"So God created man <u>in His own image</u>, in the image of God He created him..." (Gen. 1:27).*
>
> וַיִּבְרָא אֱלֹהִים אֶת־הָאָדָם
> בְּצַלְמוֹ בְּצֶלֶם אֱלֹהִים בָּרָא אֹתָם:

It was God's very own image, not a group of "images." Therefore, God's complex nature alone is the reason for the use of the word *'our'*.

Isaiah the Prophet assumes this complex nature of God in several places. In Isaiah 6:8, Isaiah quotes God as He chooses him to be a prophet of Israel:

"Who will go for Us, whom shall We send?"

אֶת־מִי אֶשְׁלַח וּמִי יֵלֶךְ־לָנוּ.

Once more in God's own counsel, God refers to Himself with a plural pronoun. Isaiah again assumes this complex unity of God's Nature in regards to our redemption:

"Come near to Me, hear this:
I have not spoken in secret from the beginning;
from the time it was, there am I;
now the Lord God and His Spirit has sent Me"
(Isaiah 48:16).

קִרְבוּ אֵלַי שִׁמְעוּ־זֹאת לֹא מֵרֹאשׁ
בַּסֵּתֶר דִּבַּרְתִּי מֵעֵת הֱיוֹתָהּ שָׁם
אֲנִי וְעַתָּה אֲדֹנָי יְהוִה שְׁלָחַנִי וְרוּחוֹ:

Who is the one "from the beginning" and the one who is always "there?" Only God alone (cp. Isaiah 48:3,5). Thus it is the Lord Himself in that verse, who is sent *by* The Lord God *and* His Spirit!

Many more portions of the Jewish Scriptures present the same truth: there is only one God, Who is complex in nature. This complexity is revealed in three persons: *Father* (Isa. 63:16; 64:8), *Son* (Isa. 9:5[6]; Prov. 30:4) and the *Holy Spirit* (Isa. 48:16; 63:10, etc. or the Spirit of God, Isa. 63:14). The Scriptures also make it clear there is only one God.

The Scriptures teach the 'Complex Nature' of God

In light of the many polytheistic religions surrounding Israel at that time, the Tanakh (Older Covenant) emphasized the oneness of God, while remaining faithful to the subtle teaching of His complex and triune nature. The New Covenant now *progressively reveals* more of this complex, triune nature, as in Matthew 28:19, etc.—**"...*immersing them in the name of the Father, the Son and the Holy Spirit...*"**, while still being faithful to the truth that there is only one God.

So, the New Covenant reveals the truth of God's complex, triune nature not to imply that there is more than one God, but to be faithful to the revelation of God's complex nature as seen in the Tanakh.

The tri-unity is not a contradiction of the oneness of God, but the best explanation of His oneness.

✡ The Tri-unity of God best explains the Tanakh's grammatical use of plural nouns and pronouns in identifying God, (Gen. 1:26; Isa. 6:8, Ecc. 12:1).

✡ The tri-unity best explains the various manifested appearances of God, (Gen. 19:24, etc.)

✡ The tri-unity best explains the use of <u>echad</u> for 'one' instead of other words for God, (Gen. 2:24, etc.)

✡ The tri-unity best explains the enigmatic and paradoxical divine nature of God (Isa. 48:16).

✡ The tri-unity best explains the Jewish mystical view of God: Kabbalah.

◆ a. Shimon Ben Yohai (2nd century): "Come and see the mystery of the word Elohim: that there are three degrees, and each degree is by itself alone, and yet they are all one, and joined together in one, and are not divided from each other."

◆ b. Zohar (the 10-11th century book on Jewish mysticism; on Deuteronomy 6:4): "*'Hear, O Israel: Jehovah our God, Jehovah is one.'* Why is there need of mentioning the name of God three times in this verse? ...The first Jehovah is the Father above. The second is the stem of Jesse, the Messiah who is to come from the family of Jesse though David. And the third on is the Way which is below (meaning the Holy Spirit who shows us the way) and these three are one."*

Thus it is not "goyisha" (gentile), but Jewish to understand God in this way.

✡ The tri-unity best explains our own "triune nature" and response to God as alluded to in Deuteronomy 6:5—

"You shall love the LORD your God with all your heart and with all your soul and with all your might."

וְאָהַבְתָּ אֵת יְהוָה אֱלֹהֶיךָ בְּכָל־לְבָבְךָ
וּבְכָל־נַפְשְׁךָ וּבְכָל־מְאֹדֶךָ:

Since we were created in His image (Gen. 1:27), we therefore are triune in nature: spirit, soul and body (*"heart...soul...might"*).

✡ The tri-unity best explains the unity of God's one truth of God's mystery nature in both Old and New Covenants, (Zechariah 14:9 and Matthew 28:19; etc.).

The tri-unity therefore, best explains the mystery nature and complex unity of God.

God's Truth is difficult for the natural mind to comprehend

A famous New Covenant scholar, Augustine of Hippo, was walking along a beach trying to understand the Tri-unity of God. As he struggled in thought, he saw a young boy digging a hole in the seashore and then run back to the water over and over taking water from the ocean and putting it in the hole. Augustine asked him, "child what are you doing?"

The boy responded "I'm trying to put the whole ocean in this hole!"

Augustine laughed and said to himself, "that's what I was trying to do, too!"

These are certainly truths hard to understand in our natural minds. Though Scripture alone reveals the true nature of God, God acknowledges that these truths are not easy to comprehend—

"For My thoughts are not your thoughts…
for as the heaven is higher than the earth, so…
my thoughts are higher than your thoughts"
(Isaiah 55:8,9).

We are to trust the testimony of scripture as the true revelation of God regarding both His nature, and His manner of reconciling sinful people to

Himself: by forgiving their sins through His atonement in Messiah Yeshua. Trust Him for who He is and for what He has done for you in Yeshua then you will have eternal life as the gift of God!

CHAPTER 9

Isn't the Virgin Birth Inconceivable?

The Virgin Birth Controversy

Of all the miracles the Bible attributes to God, it seems the 'virgin birth of Messiah' arouses the most controversy. But the same Bible that reveals God declares the virgin birth to be a historical fact. Some question whether it can be considered a scientific fact since it can not be observed nor repeated. But then what miracle can be? The virgin birth of Messiah is simply another unique and miraculous work of God!

The Issue of Miracles

For those who deny the existence of God, the issue of miracles may be irrelevant. But if you're willing to accept that there really is a God, then why should one miracle be any more difficult for God than another. "But still," some might think, "the virgin birth is hard to believe." Actually, it depends on *how big* your God is! For the One who is the

Creator of all creation, this is normal for Him. If God can do any miracle at all, then no miracle should be dismissed out of hand.

Miracle Births are Jewish!

As Jews, we should accept miracles as the *only rationale* for our existence. After all, if left to the preferences of the Egyptians and Pharaoh, the Persians and Haman, or the Nazis and Hitler, we Jews wouldn't be here at all! God promised to keep us as a people, and miraculously He has done it. And, miraculous births are a *consistent part* of Jewish history!

God decided to bless the world through a people by whom the Messiah would come (see Gen. 12:3). God chose to use Abraham and Sarah, and as the Scriptures teach us, Abraham was old, and Sarah was barren (Gen. 11:30). Thus the obvious problem is that God purposely chose to make a nation from the one couple that couldn't have kids!

Rather than this being a *problem*, this was *the point*. If the promise of God would effectively bless the world, then it would take the power of God to make it happen. And miracle of miracles, Isaac was born.

Isaac then marries Rebecca. She too was barren, but again God intervenes (Gen. 25:21). And again with Jacob, and Rachel, who was barren (Gen. 29:31) Again, God miraculously provides a miracle birth (Gen. 30:22-24).

The point is clear: the existence of the Jewish people is based upon miracle births from God. So rather than seeming abnormal, a miracle birth for the Jewish Messiah should be expected. After all, shouldn't we expect the most unusual Person in the universe to have a most unusual entrance through His birth? His unique nature would actually require it!

The Prophecy of a Virgin Birth

God actually told us to expect a virgin birth for the Messiah. As far back as the very first messianic prophecy we see this same hope:

"And I will put enmity between thee (Satan) and the woman, and between thy seed and her seed; it shall bruise thy head, and thou shalt bruise his heel" (Genesis 3:15).

God promised to remove that Serpent of old, Satan, the father of lies and anti-Semitism, through the Redeemer, who would come from *'the seed'* (זַרְעָהּ, *zarah*) of the woman. This is God's first attention-getting clue: a woman would be the instrument of Messiah's coming.

In the book of Isaiah we read of this woman again in Messiah's prophetic birth announcement:

"The Lord himself shall give you a sign:
Behold, the virgin shall conceive and bear a son,
and shall call His name Immanuel" *(Isaiah 7:14).*

לָכֵן יִתֵּן אֲדֹנָי הוּא לָכֶם אוֹת הִנֵּה הָעַלְמָה
הָרָה וְיֹלֶדֶת בֵּן וְקָרָאת שְׁמוֹ עִמָּנוּאֵל:

Some might wonder if the word *'virgin'* is an accurate translation of the Hebrew word *almah*, עַלְמָה. In the Hebrew Scriptures, the word *almah* is used seven times (Gen. 24:43; Ex. 2:8; Prov. 30:18; Ps. 68:25; Song of Sol. 1:3; 6:8). *Every time* it speaks of a *virgin*. The very root of this word, translated *secret* (עָלַם, Ps. 90:8) and *hidden* (עָלַם,

Lev. 4:13), speaks of the qualities of a virgin, as one 'hidden' from experience with men.

The Testimony of 70 Rabbis

In the second and first centuries BCE, the Hebrew Scriptures were for the first time translated into Greek by seventy Rabbis. Thus, the name of this translation has become known as the *Septuagint* (means 70). At that time they had no difficulty translating *almah* into the common Greek word for virgin, παρθένος, *parthenos*. This was *before* Yeshua's birth, and before there was any controversy over His Messiahship. Thus, these seventy rabbis were quite objective in their translation, and this is the translation that the New Covenant utilizes in describing Messiah's birth (Matthew 1:23). So, *virgin is* an accurate translation of the Hebrew text.

Some might object that another Hebrew word for *virgin* would have been used if Isaiah had meant a real "honest-to-goodness-I've-never-ever-had-sex-with-a-man" virgin. That word is *betulah,* בְּתוּלָה. It is true that *betulah* also means virgin. However, both words are synonymous, therefore either can be used. In fact, there is some question whether *betulah* would actually have been the best choice at all since it is also used for a *widow* in Joel 1:8, etc. Additionally, the eminent Jewish scholar Cyrus Gordon states that the words were synonymous and that the word *almah* is actually the best word choice for *virgin* in this situation (see "Almah in Isaiah 7:14", <u>Journal of Bible and Religion</u>, 4/1953, p. 106).

The Name "Immanuel"

You may wonder why the name "Emmanuel" is used rather than "Yeshua?" Many places in the Hebrew Scriptures tell us about Messiah, each giving us a different "name." In Isaiah 9:6 (9:5), His name is called *"Wonderful Counselor, Mighty God, Eternal Father, Prince Of Peace"*. In Jeremiah 23:6, He is called *"the Lord our Righteousness"*. In Isaiah 7:14 it is *"Immanuel"*.

As opposed to a given name, each of these names describe some quality of God's nature or character. *"Immanuel"*, עִמָּנוּ אֵל, means "God is with us." Twice in the Hebrew text (Isa. 8:8,10), it is repeated, and *"Immanuel"* is the overall theme of the portion. He also is the hope of our lives.

God will neither leave nor forsake us in our sins, for Messiah, the hope of the House of David, will come. We have, by faith in Messiah, the eternal relationship with God which our lives desperately need. For in Messiah Yeshua "God *is* with us!"

Isaiah told wicked King Ahaz that *"if you will not believe you not will be established"* (Isaiah 7:9). The same is true for each of us. Let us have faith in the wonder-working God of Israel's greatest miracle, Messiah, that we may be eternally established before Him.

CHAPTER 10

How can Yeshua possibly be the Son of David?

Among knowledgeable students of the Jewish Scriptures it is recognized that one of the necessary credentials of the true Messiah of Israel is that He be from the lineage of King David (Isaiah 7:13,14; 9:5-7; Jer. 23:5,6; etc.). Those who do not accept *Yeshua** as the Messiah argue that since He did not have an earthly father, then obviously He could not be from the lineage of David. In other words, if He was born of a virgin—as Yeshua's followers claim—then He could not also be "the son of David."

A Tale of Two Lineages

The fact of the matter is that not only is Yeshua's stepfather, Joseph, from the line of David, but His mother, Miriam, is as well. Miriam's genealogical line is traceable back to King David as recorded in Luke 3:23-31: ***"Now Yeshua Himself began His ministry at about***

*Yeshua is the Jewish way to say Jesus.

61

thirty years of age, being (as was supposed) the son of Joseph, the son of Heli, the son of Matthat, the son of Levi.... the son of Rhesa, the son of Zerubbabel, the son of Shealtiel,....the son of Nathan, the son of David, the son of Jesse..."

On the other hand, Joseph's genealogical line back to King David is recorded in Matthew 1:1-16: *"...and Jesse begot David the king. David the king begot Solomon... Josiah became the father of Jeconiah... begot Shealtiel, and Shealtiel begot Zerubbabel. Zerubbabel begot Abiud, ... Eleazar begot Matthan, and Matthan begot Jacob. And Jacob begot Joseph the husband of Miriam, of who was born Yeshua who is called Messiah."*

The text is very clear: Joseph *and* Miriam are both from the lineage of King David. Joseph came through David's most famous son, Solomon; and Miriam through Nathan, another son of David. These two lines merge again at **Shealtiel** the father of **Zerubbabel**, the governor of Judah, following the Babylonian captivity. The lines then divide again with Joseph coming from **Zerubbabel** through his son **Abiud**, and Miriam coming from **Zerubbabel** through his son **Rhesa**.

What about the Curse of Jeconiah?

According to the prophet Jeremiah, Jeconiah (a descendant of King David), had come under a curse and made David's seed through Jeconiah invalid to serve as King: *"Thus says the LORD, 'Write this man down childless, a man who will not prosper in his days; for no man of his descendants will prosper sitting on the throne of David or ruling again in Judah'"* (Jer. 22:30). Since Joseph was from Jeconiah's line, no *physical* son of Joseph could inherit the throne of David. Miriam's line, though, is untainted, thus her son could legitimately lay claim to the Davidic throne.

Although Joseph is not Yeshua's *biological* father, as his stepfather he was His legal guardian. Thus Joseph provides a patrilineal (father's side) tie to the line of David for Yeshua. This is why Joseph's genealogy is included in the New Covenant record. Since there was no earthly, *biological* father outside of the Davidic line, Yeshua had no *non-Davidic* father that would give Him any lineage other than that of King David.

On the other hand, even if only His mother was in the line of David, it would still be sufficient for Yeshua to be of Davidic lineage. Some traditional rabbis might protest that the mother's side cannot give genealogical credentials, and it is true that the biblical records are patrilineal. However, in the Scriptures there are clear exceptions regarding the right of a female to pass along the family heritage (Num. 27:1-7).

So, whether viewed from the stepfather's *legal* side, or from the mother's *biological* side, Yeshua is

In the Talmud (Jewish commentaries on the Torah), the Name *Yeshua* is irreverently rendered "*Yeshu*"- a rabbinic acrostic meaning "may his name and memory be obliterated." Even with this disrespect for Yeshua, the Talmud still affirms His Davidic lineage: **"With Yeshu however it was different, for he was connected with the government [or royalty, i.e., influential]" (Sanhedrin 43a).**

"the son of David," and the authorized Messiah of Israel. In fact, since the Messiah was prophesied to be "virgin-born" (see Isa. 7:13,14), this is the very way the lineage would have had to have been worked out. The fact that the true Messiah not only had to be a son of David, but virgin-born as well, narrows down the field quite a bit. So, other than Yeshua, what legitimate claimants are there for the position?

David's Son, David's Lord

Paradoxically, Messiah the son of David was also to be the Son of God—in fact, Messiah was actually to be the *Mighty God* (Isa. 9:5, אֵל גִּבּוֹר, *El Gibbor*). The son of David was not only to reign from David's throne over all Israel, but to have ultimate authority over all of the peoples of the world (see Isa. 2:1-4; 11:10; 49:6). Yeshua again is the only claimant with the proper credentials.

In Psalm 2 David wrote, ***"Kiss the son, lest he be angry, and ye perish in the way, For his wrath will soon be kindled. Blessed are all they that take refuge in him"*** (v.12). *"Kiss the Son"* (נַשְּׁקוּ־בַר) meant to give homage to the Son, as symbolized in kissing the ring of the King. Yeshua is therefore the only One who has *authentic* as well as *authorized* authority over each of our lives. He is the one, true Son of God to whom we are to give due homage. Yeshua is the one and only Son of David who can give true security to our people for today, and for eternity, even as was prophesied in Jeremiah 23:5,6:

הִנֵּה יָמִים בָּאִים נְאֻם־יְהֹוָה
וַהֲקִמֹתִי לְדָוִד צֶמַח צַדִּיק וּמָלַךְ מֶלֶךְ וְהִשְׂכִּיל וְעָשָׂה
מִשְׁפָּט וּצְדָקָה בָּאָרֶץ: בְּיָמָיו תִּוָּשַׁע יְהוּדָה וְיִשְׂרָאֵל
יִשְׁכֹּן לָבֶטַח וְזֶה־שְּׁמוֹ אֲשֶׁר־יִקְרְאוֹ יְהֹוָה צִדְקֵנוּ:

*"'Behold, the days are coming,' says the LORD,
'that I will raise up for David a righteous Branch;
a King shall reign and prosper, and execute
judgment and righteousness in the earth.
In His days Judah will be saved,
and Israel will dwell securely.
And this is His name by which He will be called:
THE LORD OUR RIGHTEOUSNESS.'"*

One day Israel as a people will enjoy this
security when we, as a nation, return to the son of
David, Messiah Yeshua the Lord, even as prophesied in Hosea 3:5.

אַחַר יָשֻׁבוּ בְּנֵי יִשְׂרָאֵל וּבִקְשׁוּ אֶת־יְהֹוָה
אֱלֹהֵיהֶם וְאֵת דָּוִד מַלְכָּם וּפָחֲדוּ אֶל־יְהֹוָה וְאֶל־טוּבוֹ
בְּאַחֲרִית הַיָּמִים:

*"Afterward the children of Israel shall return and
seek the LORD their God and David their king.
They shall fear the LORD and His goodness
in the latter days."*

Today as individuals, each of us can return to
our true Lord and King, Yeshua, and *be saved, dwell
securely* and receive His *goodness*. Let us *"give
homage to the Son"* by yielding to His authority
through obedience to His Word. As we acknowledge our sins and depend on His atonement, trusting
in His sacrifice, we can rest knowing He is *THE
LORD OUR RIGHTEOUSNESS.*

CHAPTER 11

Why Would the True Jewish Messiah Have to Come Twice?

To some it appears that followers of Yeshua* are at least in denial, if not avoiding 'the painful truth' by believing in "the Second Coming." "Why would it be necessary for Messiah to come twice," the doubtful ask. "Didn't He get it right the first time? And, if he is the Jewish Messiah, as you claim, where in the Jewish Scriptures does it say anything about two comings of the Messiah?"

Two pictures of Messiah: To reign, yet to be rejected

The issue of "two comings" of the Messiah is neither non-Jewish nor particularly unusual to Jewish thought. For two millennia the rabbinical community has been discussing, pondering and conjecturing the possible ways to resolve paradoxical and seemingly contradictory references to the Messiah in the Jewish Scriptures.

On one hand, the Scriptures present a picture of

Yeshua is the Jewish way to say Jesus.

the Messiah reigning:

"The kings of the earth take their stand
against the LORD and His Messiah…
The LORD laughs at them…saying, 'I have
installed My King on Zion'" (Psalm 2:2-4).

יִתְיַצְּבוּ מַלְכֵי־אֶרֶץ...עַל־יהוָה וְעַל־מְשִׁיחוֹ
...יִשְׂחָק אֲדֹנָי... וַאֲנִי נָסַכְתִּי מַלְכִּי עַל־צִיּוֹן

"Behold, days are coming, says the LORD, that I
will raise up for David a righteous Branch, and a
King shall reign and prosper" (Jeremiah 23:5).

הִנֵּה יָמִים בָּאִים נְאֻם־יהוָה וַהֲקִמֹתִי
לְדָוִד צֶמַח צַדִּיק וּמָלַךְ מֶלֶךְ וְהִשְׂכִּיל

In these portions, and in many others (Genesis 49:10; Numbers 24:17; Ps. 45:6,7; Ps. 110:1-7; Isaiah 2:1-4; 11:10; Zechariah 14:3,4,16, etc.), Messiah is pictured as ruling and reigning over the enemies of God. This is a time of peace and joy, Israel is the chief of nations again, and the Lord and the Davidic throne are gloriously established in Jerusalem.

But alongside this exalted scene, there is also the picture of Messiah rejected:

"And the Messiah will be cut off
and will have nothing" (Daniel 9:26).

יִכָּרֵת מָשִׁיחַ וְאֵין לוֹ

"He had no beauty or majesty to attract us to
Him, nothing in His appearance that we should
be attracted to Him. He was a man of sorrows
and familiar with suffering. Surely, He took
upon Himself our griefs and sorrows, yet we
considered Him stricken by God and afflicted

by Him. We did not esteem Him... Who of His generation considered Him? For He was cut off from the land of the living for the transgressions of my people to whom the stroke was due" (Isaiah 53:2-8; the full text of Isaiah 53 is on page 116).

"I am a worm and not a man, scorned by men and despised by the people. All who see Me mock me and hurl insults... you lay Me at the door of death...they have pierced My hands and my feet..." (Psalm 22:6-16 [22:7-17])

וְאָנֹכִי תוֹלַעַת וְלֹא־אִישׁ

כָּאֲרִי יָדַי וְרַגְלָי

In these portions and many others (Isaiah 49:7; 50:6; Psalm 69:4-22; Zechariah 11:12; etc.) Messiah is seen as rejected and suffering in innocence for the sins of others. Therefore, two different works of Messiah are presented in Scripture: 1) He will suffer and die for sins; 2) He will reign and rule in peace.

TRAditionAl Jewish ideAs REGARdiNG the two woRks of the MessiAh

These two, contrasting, Scriptural pictures of the Messiah have brought about various Jewish theories of how the Messiah could both reign, and yet be rejected; a celebrated victor, while also a sacrificial victim.

The rabbinical explanations included:

✡ a *Resurrected Messiah;*
✡ a *Leper Messiah;*
✡ *Two Messiahs*—Messiah *Son of Joseph*, who would innocently suffer as the Patriarch Joseph suffered, and Messiah *Son of David*, who will

reign as David reigned;

✡ a *Beggar Messiah*; etc.

These ideas are quite prevalent in the rabbinical literature (Sukkot 52a,b; Gen. Rabbah LXXV, 6; XCV; XCIX, 2; S.S. Rabbah II, 4; Num. Rabbah XIV, 1; Sepher Sippurim Noraim 9a-b, 10b). Within all these ideas, we see traditional Jewish scholarship struggling to understand these two very different biblical pictures of the Jewish Messiah.

Two comings of Messiah revealed!

Hosea the Prophet speaks to the subject as well, as he presents God speaking to a wayward Israel:

"Then I will go back to My place until they admit their guilt and seek my face; in their misery they will earnestly seek Me"
(Hosea 5:15).

אֵלֵךְ אָשׁוּבָה אֶל־מְקוֹמִי עַד אֲשֶׁר־יֶאְשְׁמוּ
וּבִקְשׁוּ פָנָי בַּצַּר לָהֶם יְשַׁחֲרֻנְנִי׃

We see God offended at Israel's sins and going *back to [His] place (Heaven) until they admit guilt.* The implication is that *when* they **admit their guilt",** *then* He will return to them. This is clearly stated in Israel's response to the Lord's departure from them:

"Let us acknowledge the LORD; let us press on to acknowledge Him. As surely as the sun rises, He will appear; He will come to us like the winter rains, like the spring rains that water the earth" (Hosea 6:3).

וְנֵדְעָה נִרְדְּפָה לָדַעַת אֶת־יהוָה כְּשַׁחַר נָכוֹן
מוֹצָאוֹ וְיָבוֹא כַגֶּשֶׁם לָנוּ כְּמַלְקוֹשׁ יוֹרֶה אָרֶץ׃

Though God had left, they had confidence He

would also certainly return. In the Lord's statement there was hope that their admission of guilt would bring about His return.

In light of all this discussion it should surprise no one that the Messiah Himself would come and clarify these apparently contradictory pictures of His work. Similar to the portion in Hosea, Yeshua says to Israel:

"You shall not see me again until you say 'Blessed is He that comes in the name of the Lord"
(Matthew 23:39).

Following Yeshua's death, burial, resurrection and ascension (going back to His place), Peter proclaims to the Jewish crowds in Jerusalem:

"Repent, then, and turn to God, so that your sins may be wiped away, that the times of refreshing may come from the Lord, and that He may send the Messiah, who has been appointed for you, even Jesus. He must remain in Heaven until the time comes for God to restore everything, as He promised long ago in the holy prophets" (Acts 3:19-21).

The New Covenant revelation regarding the two works of Messiah is not new. It is a clarification and fulfillment of what the Jewish Scriptures prophesied: Messiah would come to die for our sins, be raised from the dead, go back to His place, and return when our people acknowledge their guilt and call out to Him. Just as Joseph was at first rejected by his brothers, then later accepted (Genesis 37, 50), and as Moses was first rejected by Israel, then later accepted (Exodus 2:14, 4:31), so Messiah would be rejected and then later accepted by Israel:

"They will look unto Me (God)
whom they have pierced, and mourn for Him as
one mourns for an only son" (Zechariah 12:10).

וְהִבִּיטוּ אֵלַי אֵת אֲשֶׁר־דָּקָרוּ
וְסָפְדוּ עָלָיו כְּמִסְפֵּד עַל־הַיָּחִיד

The return of the Messiah is mentioned many times in the New Covenant (Matt. 24-25; 1 Thess. 1:10; 4:13-5:9; Rev. 22, etc.). This is because the Jewish Scriptures will be fulfilled *in every detail.* Just as Messiah had to suffer and die for sins, so He will also return to reign and bring peace. So look to Him now, trust in the atonement He made by His death for your sins, and receive the new life that He gives to all who come to Him!

המברך את עמו ישראל בשלום

CHAPTER 12

If Jesus is The Jewish Messiah, Then Why Don't Most Jews Believe in Him?

It seems to many rather strange, that the Jewish Messiah could have come and comparatively so few Jews believe it. Many times the question actually sounds more like this: "So, with all the scholars and rabbis searching to discover the Messiah, how is it that you're the only genius to figure this out?"

The number of Jewish people around the world who presently believe in Yeshua* ranges from 200,000 to 1 million, perhaps more. Though this number is not insignificant, it's still not the majority of our people. For many there's the idea that 'truth' is determined by a majority vote. As much as this may play a role in the politics of men, this has little to do with the truth of God.

In the Jewish Scriptures (Tanakh), the prophet Isaiah declares that most Jewish people would not

Yeshua is the Jewish way to say Jesus.

72

recognize the Messiah when He would initially come:

> *"Who has believed our report? To whom has the arm of the Lord been revealed? For He grew up before Him as a tender shoot, as a root out of dry ground; He would have no majesty that would attract us, nor any beauty that we would desire Him. He is despised and forsaken of men, a man of sorrows, and acquainted with grief, and we hid as it were our faces from Him; He was despised and we esteemed Him not."* (Isaiah 53:1-3; the full text of Isaiah 53 is on page 116).

God knew and revealed to Isaiah what may not seem all that hard to figure out: Most people don't want God's way of salvation—even religious people! In fact, that's exactly what Isaiah goes on to say:

> *"All we like sheep have gone astray, each one has turned his own way; but the Lord has laid on Him the iniquity of us all"*
> (Isaiah 53:6).

Though the Messiah would be our sin-bearer, the true Messiah would *not* be accepted but be rejected by the majority of the Jewish people when He would first come. Isaiah makes this matter crystal clear by further stating:

> *"The remnant shall return, even the remnant of Jacob to the Mighty God"*
> (Isaiah 10:21; see also Isaiah 9:5[6]).

שְׁאָר יָשׁוּב שְׁאָר יַעֲקֹב אֶל־אֵל גִּבּוֹר:

We recognize then that a "remnant" (שְׁאָר), a very

small portion of the whole nation, would believe and make teshuvah/repentance. Only this remnant would "return to the Mighty God." This is a prediction fulfilled in the Jewish people (like myself) who have come to believe in Yeshua. Similarly, in the New Covenant when it discusses and compares the present situation of the Jewish people with their condition in time of Elijah the prophet, this truth is reiterated:

"Even so, then, at this present time also there is a remnant according to the election of grace" (Romans 11:5).

Though the Scriptures make it clear, some will still wonder how the Rabbis could have "missed it." The answer is, the Messiah that God promised and sent was not the Messiah the world or the rabbis were looking for. They wanted a Messiah who would forcibly remove Roman domination over Israel, and return Israel to its former glory. But in God's eyes, our true problem is not external, but internal: the dominating power of sin in the souls of all men and women, both Jewish and non-Jewish. Thus to satisfy God's justice, and spare mankind the punishment we deserve, the purpose of Messiah's first coming was to die for sins. And rather than approve the traditional judgments of the rabbis, He insisted that the religious leaders of Israel would have to repent as well! That was intolerable and too much for the rabbinical leaders, and so Messiah was rejected. Though many accepted Yeshua as the Messiah, the majority of the Jewish people and the Rabbis did not to respond favorably to Yeshua, as it was predicted.

But the Prophets also predicted there will come

a time when our people will *nationally* come to believe in Him.

"I will pour upon the house of David and the inhabitants of Jerusalem the Spirit of grace and supplications; and they shall look on Me whom they have pierced, and mourn for Him as one mourns for an only son"
(Zechariah 12:10).

וְשָׁפַכְתִּי עַל־בֵּית דָּוִיד וְעַל יוֹשֵׁב
יְרוּשָׁלַם רוּחַ חֵן וְתַחֲנוּנִים וְהִבִּיטוּ אֵלַי
אֵת אֲשֶׁר־דָּקָרוּ וְסָפְדוּ עָלָיו כְּמִסְפֵּד
עַל־הַיָּחִיד וְהָמֵר עָלָיו כְּהָמֵר עַל־הַבְּכוֹר:

"The stone which the builders rejected shall become the chief of the corner!"
(Psalms 118:22).

אֶבֶן מָאֲסוּ הַבּוֹנִים הָיְתָה לְרֹאשׁ פִּנָּה:

One day our people will trust in Yeshua as their Messiah and King.

Just as it was foretold, *today* a "remnant of Israel" believes in the Messiah. You can be part of that remnant, if you will acknowledge Yeshua for what the Tanakh and New Covenant declare Him to be: the Messiah and Savior of our people.

CHAPTER 13

Aren't Christians and The New Testament Anti-Semitic?

Because Jewish history is filled with persecution by many so-called Christians, Jewish people can often ask questions that presume guilt. "Isn't the New Testament anti-Semitic? Doesn't it teach Christians to hate Jews? What about 'Christian' anti-Semitism and the Holocaust?" On the surface these may appear to be valid questions, but to some, the facts may be quite surprising.

The New Testament is Jewish?

It's a shock to many people when they discover just how *Jewish* the New Testament actually is! Jeremiah the prophet foretold that God would give the New Testament (or New Covenant, *Brit Chadasha* in Hebrew, בְּרִית חֲדָשָׁה) to our people:

"Behold, the days are coming when I will make a New Covenant with the House of Israel and with the House of Judah. It is not like the covenant that I made with your fathers in the day I took them by the hand to bring them out of the land of Egypt, a covenant which they broke, though I was a husband to them, says the Lord…for I will forgive their iniquities and remember their sins no more" (Jer. 31:31- 34).

הִנֵּה יָמִים בָּאִים נְאֻם־יְהוָה וְכָרַתִּי
אֶת־בֵּית יִשְׂרָאֵל וְאֶת־בֵּית יְהוּדָה בְּרִית חֲדָשָׁה:
לֹא כַבְּרִית אֲשֶׁר כָּרַתִּי אֶת־אֲבוֹתָם בְּיוֹם הֶחֱזִיקִי
בְיָדָם לְהוֹצִיאָם מֵאֶרֶץ מִצְרָיִם אֲשֶׁר־הֵמָּה
הֵפֵרוּ אֶת־בְּרִיתִי וְאָנֹכִי בָּעַלְתִּי בָם נְאֻם־יְהוָה:
כִּי אֶסְלַח לַעֲוֹנָם וּלְחַטָּאתָם לֹא אֶזְכָּר־עוֹד:

The New Covenant is what Messiah Yeshua* initiated when He died to make atonement for sins. It is His death that established the basis of the New Covenant relationship between God and His people: the forgiveness of sins for all who will believe.

As a young Jewish man growing up in New York, I thought the New Testament was a combination religious rulebook for Gentiles, and an instruction manual for anti-Semitism.

Upon reading it for myself, I was surprised to find that the New Covenant is actually the Lord's love letter to those who seek Him.

Yeshua is the Jewish way to say Jesus.

The Jewish Messiah's Love

As far as being a cause for anti-Semitism, this could never happen for those who have read it's pages and believed its words. In this Jewish book, Yeshua is presented as "the King of the Jews." He is shown crying over Jerusalem (Luke 19:41), fulfilling the Law and the prophets (Matthew 5:17), and identifying *only* with the Jewish people in His daily activities (Matt. 10:5,6; 15:24). How could any so-called follower of Yeshua claim to have the King of *the Jews* in their hearts, and also hate the Jewish people? Absurd! Rather, true Gentile followers of the Jewish Messiah love the Jewish people.

The life and teachings of Yeshua give no justification for any kind of hatred, let alone hatred of His Jewish people...

"For the love of Messiah controls" them
(2 Cor. 5:14).

It is better said that *anti-Semitism is proof of the ignorance of those who disobey Messiah and His teachings.*

True Followers of Jesus Love the Jewish People

The experience of the Holocaust of the 1930's and 40's, as well as other anti-Semitic persecutions, are often thought of as an expression of 'Christian' hatred toward the Jewish people. The Holocaust was no such thing at all. Gentile governments have routinely used and abused the label of religion in a futile attempt to justify their pragmatic and evil national interests. In the Hebrew Scriptures as well, the same truth is revealed:

Anti-Semitism is anti-God (see Psalm 83:1-5).

* *"The Hiding Place"* by Corrie Ten Boom evidences theses facts.

78

True Gentile followers of Messiah were persecuted, imprisoned and murdered by the Nazis for helping the Jews in their areas.* Jewish believers in Messiah were killed as quickly as the other Jews. There was nothing about the vicious hatred toward the Jewish people that represented anything taught in the New Covenant, or by any faithful follower of Messiah Yeshua.

The Real Cause of Anti-Semitism

The New Covenant teaches us how the Jewish Messiah came to resolve a problem that is universal: the problem of sin. Sin, the power that spurred the Nazis is essentially the same problem *all* people have—rebellion against God. This sin of problem ends when a person, any person, acknowledges their sin to God, and places their trust in Messiah Yeshua.

I once had the opportunity to speak at a businessmen's breakfast where I shared the message of Good News. I invited the people there to respond to God's love and forgiveness in the Jewish Messiah. Of those who responded, I remember one businessman who burst into tears. Up to that point he had been an anti-Semite. But now he was convinced of his sinfulness and wanted to repent. After we prayed he mentioned that he was stunned to have heard the message of forgiveness and new life in the *Jewish* Messiah from a *Jewish* man! It became clear to him that his anti-Semitic feelings were just one symptom of his rebellion to God— affirming the scriptural truth that anti-Semitism is anti-God, and anti-Messiah.

As evil and offensive as anti-Semitism is, all sin

is offensive to God. Though some sins are not nearly so blatant, God is aware of them all. All who sin need to repent in order to be forgiven and cleansed of their sins. The message of Good News is for all who will trust in Israel's Messiah and the Savior of the world, Yeshua.

CHAPTER 14

Why the Holocaust?
A Biblical View
of a Horror in History

"Bialystok"

I cried when I saw the name "Bialystok." I didn't expect to, but perhaps it was my reaction to the previous two hours of horrors at the Holocaust Museum in Washington, D.C. My mother and her immediate family, the Hirshbeins, moved to the States from Bialystok, Poland before the war. Those who escaped survived; the rest of my family perished as the Nazis eradicated the Jewish community of Bialystok.

This was not the first Holocaust in Jewish history, and, sadly, it won't be the last. Zechariah predicts a future period even more horrible, if it can be imagined, for our Jewish people (see Zech. 12-14). About 1/3 of all Jewish people were murdered during the Nazi regime; Zechariah prophesies that during this next Holocaust, 2/3 of the Jewish people will be lost! (Zech. 13:8).

Why, O God, Why? Why Holocausts?

The Scriptures are clear regarding the reason for anti-Semitism in general, and Holocausts in particular: *Spiritual Warfare.*

For those unaware of the idea of 'spiritual warfare', please review portions of the Tanakh (the Jewish Scriptures) that teach on this vital subject. Some of these are Job 1-2; Zechariah 3, and especially Daniel 10, as well as others noted below from Old and New Covenants alike.

Without minimizing individual moral accountability, the Scriptures teach that there *is* a Devil, 'Satan' (שָׂטָן, see Job 1-2; Zechariah 3, etc.), and that he is in rebellion against God. Satan manipulates, influences, and even controls the spiritually willing, the foolish, and evil dupes (i.e., Hitler).

A. Satan's Goal: Replace God

The Scriptures inform us that this enemy of God, Satan (Hebrew for "adversary"), is waging an active, yet often subtle war against God. And though it may seem more futile than, as they say, 'a one-legged man trying to kick down a steel door', Satan is wickedly working to defeat and dethrone God (see Isaiah 14:12-14).

B. Satan's Plan: 'Prove' God is a Liar

God cannot lie (Titus 1:2). The Devil's plan is to attempt to make God a liar by nullifying God's promises regarding the Jewish people, and the Jewish Messiah. God has promised that the Jewish people will always exist:

"Thus says the LORD, Who gives the sun for light by day and the fixed order of the moon and the

stars for light by night, Who stirs up the sea so that its waves roar; the LORD of hosts is His name:
'If this fixed order departs from before Me,' declares the LORD, 'Then the offspring of Israel also will cease from being a nation before Me forever.'
Thus says the LORD, 'If the heavens above can be measured and the foundations of the earth searched out below, then I will also cast off all the offspring of Israel for all that they have done,' declares the LORD" (Jer. 31:35-37).

In other words, you first have to remove the solar system before you can completely remove Israel as a people before God.

The purpose of Israel is to be God's conduit for the world's blessing (Gen. 12:3; 22:18; Gal. 3:14). Through Israel would come Messiah, the world's Savior, who will ultimately be Satan's destroyer.

C. Satan's Activity: Stop Jewish Survival

Therefore Satan is trying to nullify the Jews as a people using two strategies:

1. Stop the Jews from living!

The first, and the most obvious strategy, is recorded in Psalm 83:1-5:
"Your foes rear their heads... They plot against those You cherish. 'Come,' they say, 'let us destroy them as a nation, that the name of Israel will be remembered no more.'"

אָמְרוּ לְכוּ וְנַכְחִידֵם מִגּוֹי
וְלֹא־יִזָּכֵר שֵׁם־יִשְׂרָאֵל עוֹד:

Simply put, 'destroy the Jews, and prove God to be a liar.' For if God can't keep His people that He promised to keep, then no one can trust any of His other promises or Scripture. And if Satan can destroy Israel as a people, he therefore proves himself to be greater than God.

> # The Bible teaches that anti-Semitism is anti-God.

This accounts for the Pharaohs, Hamans, Herods and Hitlers throughout the centuries. Though merely tools of Satan they are in no way excused of their culpability. We are all responsible for our decisions and actions regardless of what influences us in those actions.

2. Stop the Jews from living as Jews!

The second, albeit more subtle strategy is to make Jewish identity odious, or at least irrelevant to the Jewish people and to others. By making Jewish people not want to remain Jewish, Israel would cease to be an identifiable nation before God.

In the book of Esther, Esther heeds Mordecai's bad advice, *"Don't reveal you're a Jew" (Esther 2:10).* Only when she abandoned that bad advice and revealed her Jewish identity was catastrophe averted.

This same bad advice has been relived by many of our people in every generation. Take, for example, Hellenism in Judah in the early Second Century BCE. Some Jews, in order to fit into the Gentile world, actually had themselves surgically *un*circumcised! Today "being Jewish" is so poorly understood that many Jews make no attempt to maintain their heritage.

The shame of it all is that there are even some Jewish believers in Yeshua* that don't maintain their Jewish identity. In some cases, they didn't value their Jewishness before they came to faith in Yeshua. Sometimes Jewish believers in Yeshua are told (and they foolishly believe) that as followers of Yeshua, they are no longer Jews. In any case by not identifying as Jews, as believers they play right into Satan's plan: stop the Jewish people from existing as an identifiable people. In so doing, Jewish believers make faith in Yeshua appear repulsive to the general Jewish community, and unknowingly work against the very testimony of God's faithfulness in the identifiable existence of the Jewish people (see Jer. 31:36)! That some Jewish believers in Yeshua consider themselves no longer Jews is astounding in light of the teaching in the New Covenant.

Though an emissary for God to the Gentiles, Paul knew what was at stake in maintaining his Jewish identity: the very faithfulness of God. Would the Good News of Yeshua that he proclaimed to Gentiles mean **"God had rejected his people?"** *(Romans 11:1)*. His answer, **"By no means. For I _am_ an Israelite, a descendant of Abraham, from the tribe of Benjamin. God will not reject his people He foreknew"** *(Romans 11:1,2).*

Every Jewish believer who states *"I _am_ an Israelite"* or *"I _am_ a Jew,"* as opposed to "I *was* a Jew" or "I am a *former* Jew," confirms with Paul, that God is keeping His people (see Acts 22:3). God is faithful. Yeshua is Israel's hope, not its destroyer!

We Jewish believers, for the sake of the faithfulness of God, and in light of the raging

Yeshua is the Jewish way to say Jesus. 85

spiritual warfare, have a <u>responsibility</u> to *maintain our Jewish identity*. Along with this responsibility, we also have a liberty as how to express our Jewishness (just as the larger Jewish community enjoys its liberty in the various expressions of Jewish identity). But our lives must in some way declare *"Am Yisrael Chai b'Yeshua HaMashiach - the People of Israel live in Yeshua the Messiah!"* Especially, in light of who Yeshua is in this spiritual warfare.

D. SATAN'S DESTROYER: THE JEWISH MESSIAH

God promised that the Redeemer of mankind, the destroyer of Satan, would be the Messiah of Israel (see Gen. 3:15).

1. STOP MESSIAH FROM COMING!

Satan would need to stop this Redeemer from coming and fulfilling His mission. We see how this dovetails with his previous ploy, since the Redeemer was promised to come through the Jewish people (Genesis 12:3; 22:18; 49:10; Isa. 11:10; 49:5-7). Satan is no fuzzy-minded sentimentalist, but an utterly evil pragmatist. If he destroys the Jews, he keeps his own destruction from ever coming. This accounts for the overt anti-Semitism in the Older Covenant through Pharaoh, Haman, etc. In a sense, this would provide a "two-fer" for Satan: destroy God's conduit for Messiah's coming (the Jews) and make God a liar at the same time. Not only had God promised Jewish survival (Jeremiah 31:35-37) but also that through the Jews the Messiah would come into the world (see Micah 5:2; Isa 7:14; 9:5-7, etc.)

But despite Satan's attempts, Messiah was born and died for our sins and was raised from the dead! On this point we know Satan has failed. But if Satan failed, then why, even after Messiah's resurrection, does anti-Semitism continue today?

At the present time *"the devil prowls like a roaring lion looking for someone to devour" (1 Peter 5:8)*. But when Messiah returns to earth to restore the Davidic kingdom, He will then have Satan bound for a 1000 years (Rev. 20:1-3). Afterwards, Satan will be *"thrown in the Lake of Fire"* forever (Rev. 20:10)! The linchpin to this future victory of God is the survival of the Jewish people, for the return of the Lord is dependent upon the repentance of Israel. This is why Yeshua said to our people...

"You will not see me again until you say, 'Baruch Haba B'Shem Adonai --Blessed is He that comes in the Name of the Lord'"
(Matthew 23:39).

Yeshua will not return to reign on the Davidic throne and remove the adversary, Satan, until the Jewish people acknowledge Him as King. Typically, David could not rule over all of Israel and remove the adversaries until the people accepted him as king (2 Samuel 5:1-5). Peter reiterates this point when he proclaims to the Jewish people...

"Repent and turn to God, that your sins might be wiped away, in order that the times of refreshing might come from the Lord, and that He might send the Messiah, who has been appointed for you— even Yeshua. He <u>must remain</u> in Heaven until the time comes for God to restore everything, as He promised..." (Acts 3:19-21).

The return of Yeshua who will "restore everything" (*"the times of refreshing"*) as well as the destruction of Satan, depends on the Jewish people *"repenting and returning to God"*—the return of Yeshua to reign on earth depends on the repentance of Israel.

2. Stop Messiah from coming again!

Therefore, Satan is desperately trying to stop the return of the Messiah. This is why Satan is doing all he can to destroy the Jewish people. At the same time he is trying to make faith in Yeshua so alien and repugnant that no self-respecting Jew, let alone the nation, would ever desire to repent and trust in Him! It also explains why few Jewish or Gentile congregations who believe in Yeshua endeavor to bring the Good News to the Jewish people. It seems so hard to share the "Good News" with our people. Tragically, this plays into the present plan of Satan: stop Israel from recognizing their Messiah, Satan's destroyer, so He can't return.

Why holocausts? Because of spiritual warfare. Therefore let us *"fight the good fight"* (1 Tim. 6:12). I'm asking all Bible believing congregations to:

✡ observe Holocaust Remembrance Day
✡ *"pray for the peace of Jerusalem"* (Ps. 122:6)
✡ do all they can to show the love of Messiah to Jewish people.

I'm also asking for all Jews to live as "present tense" Jews, and also come to know the greatest Jewish blessing, Messiah Yeshua.

May Israel soon say, *"Baruch Haba B'Shem Adonai—Blessed is He who comes in the Name of the Lord!"*

מְגִילַת אֵיכָה

CHAPTER 14

WHAT IS THE JEWISH WAY TO GOD?

ISAIAH AVENUE!
THE STEPS TO GOD
FROM
THE JEWISH SCRIPTURES

The Lord God of Israel desires to provide us with rest and peace through an eternal relationship with Himself. The five following principles from the Prophet Isaiah help us to obtain that relationship with God.

1) SINNERS beFORE GOD
"All of us have become like one who is unclean,
and all our righteous acts are like filthy rags;
we all shrivel up like a leaf, and like the wind our
sins sweep us away" (Isaiah 64:5[6]).

וַנְּהִי כַטָּמֵא כֻּלָּנוּ וּכְבֶגֶד עִדִּים כָּל־צִדְקֹתֵינוּ
וַנָּבֶל כֶּעָלֶה כֻּלָּנוּ וַעֲוֹנֵנוּ כָּרוּחַ יִשָּׂאֻנוּ׃

Though we may judge ourselves by relative

standards—"I'm as good as the next person" or "I'm no worse than other people"—God judges each of us by absolute standards of Himself and His Law. *"You shall be holy as the Lord your God is holy" (Lev. 19:2)*. By His holy standards, we are all moral failures. It's not that you aren't a nice person or forget Mother's Day. But you and the next person still fall short of God's standards. By the way, every Rabbi, Priest, and Minister have the same problem. Psalm 14:3 declares, *"there is none that does good, no not one."* So, no pointing a finger, or throwing the first *or* second stone at anyone else. We all have the same great problem.

2) Separation from God

"Surely the arm of the Lord is not too short to save, nor His ear too dull to hear.
But your iniquities have separated you
from your God; your sins have hidden His face
from you so that He will not hear"
(Isaiah 59:1,2).

הֵן לֹא־קָצְרָה יַד־יְהוָה מֵהוֹשִׁיעַ
וְלֹא־כָבְדָה אָזְנוֹ מִשְּׁמוֹעַ:
כִּי אִם־עֲוֺנֹתֵיכֶם הָיוּ מַבְדִּלִים
בֵּינֵכֶם לְבֵין אֱלֹהֵיכֶם וְחַטֹּאותֵיכֶם
הִסְתִּירוּ פָנִים מִכֶּם מִשְּׁמוֹעַ:

The result of our sin is a broken relationship with God. Now you may pray and even fast, but the Scripture is clear: *"He will not hear."*

It's as if I stole money from you, and then have the "chutzpah" (nerve/gall) to come and ask you for a loan! The response from you would be, "first let's deal with the past offense, then we can consider your present or future needs." God wants to bless you, but your sins separate you from Him and must be dealt with first. If this separation continues to our death, it becomes a judgment of *everlasting* separation from God. You must understand that this fact breaks God's heart; because He truly loves you and desires you to have everlasting life with Him. That's why the story doesn't end here, but continues on with Good News for your life.

3) Salvation in God
"All we like sheep have gone astray, each of us have turned to his own way; but the Lord has laid on Him [Messiah] the sins of us all"
(Isaiah 53:6)

כֻּלָּנוּ כַּצֹּאן תָּעִינוּ אִישׁ לְדַרְכּוֹ פָּנִינוּ
וַיהוָה הִפְגִּיעַ בּוֹ אֵת עֲוֹן כֻּלָּנוּ:

Though there's no deed that we can perform to save ourselves, God has provided the way of salvation and forgiveness. He promised to send the Messiah to die for our sins, as an atonement or payment for our sins; because He loves you and me. In the New Covenant, Messiah Yeshua* states as well, *"I give my life as a ransom for many"* (Matt. 20:28). This is the salvation and right relationship that God freely offers.

4) Savior is God
"To us a child is born, to us a son is given, and the government shall be upon His shoulders. And He will be called Wonderful Counselor, Mighty God, Everlasting Father, Prince of Peace"
(Isaiah 9:5/6).

כִּי־יֶלֶד יֻלַּד־לָנוּ בֵּן נִתַּן־לָנוּ וַתְּהִי הַמִּשְׂרָה
עַל־שִׁכְמוֹ וַיִּקְרָא שְׁמוֹ פֶּלֶא יוֹעֵץ אֵל גִּבּוֹר
אֲבִיעַד שַׂר־שָׁלוֹם:

God Himself could alone provide the perfect sacrifice for sins, for He alone is perfect. What amazing love and humility, that the Mighty God of Israel would be born a babe, live as a Jewish man, and die as our perfect atonement. Messiah Yeshua is "Adonai," the Lord.

5) Steadfast upon God

"You will keep in perfect peace him whose mind is steadfast, because he trusts in You" (Isaiah 26:3).

יֵצֶר סָמוּךְ תִּצֹּר שָׁלוֹם שָׁלוֹם כִּי בְךָ בָטוּחַ:

God has provided atonement in the Messiah. It is in this provision from God that we are to trust. Our simple, but sincere acknowledgement of our sins, and our trust in Messiah Yeshua as our atonement, our Savior and Lord, is all that God requires. Upon trusting in Messiah, He provides us *"perfect peace"* and eternal life.

Like Abraham, you can have a right relationship with God by faith in what He alone can and has provided:

"Abram believed God, and He credited it to him as righteousness" (Genesis 15:6).

וְהֶאֱמִן בַּיהוָה וַיַּחְשְׁבֶהָ לּוֹ צְדָקָה:

If you too believe God and what His Scripture has declared and promised, then you too are made right with God. Trust in Israel's Messiah and the world's Savior, Yeshua!

They Found The Answer!

Jewish Stories
of
Jewish Faith

In The Shadow of the Swastika

Frieda Roos, Holocaust Survivor

I was born and raised in Amsterdam, Holland, of Jewish parents. They never talked about God, and I had never been in a synagogue except for my brother's wedding. For me, Yom Kippur meant a day off from school, and the only Jewish events that took place in our home were the Bar-Mitzvahs of my two brothers! Still, we considered ourselves very Jewish. In my teenage years I had a Gentile boyfriend, and since my parents had forbidden me from seeing him because he was a Gentile, we often sneaked into a local Catholic church to be together. I was always impressed by the paintings there of the crucifixion and moved by the sadness expressed in the face of Jesus, as the artist perceived the magnitude of that event. But the times were soon to change: I would become a fugitive, running for my very life.

From Singer to Survivor

The Lord blessed me with a soprano singing voice, and after studying at the Amsterdam Conservatory, I embarked on a career that led me to sing the Dutch version of Disney's Snow White. From there my work included: the Grand Diploma in the Geneva, Switzerland World Contest; the role of the Forestbird in Wagner's Siegfried with the Bayreuth Festspiel Haus; a Command performance of Verdi's Requiem for the Queen of Holland; many live broadcasts and concert performances; and oratorios like Handel's "The Messiah" and the many beautiful Christian cantatas by Bach. But, when the Second World War began, my singing career ended abruptly. I was immediately disqualified from any and all regular concert performances because I was Jewish. The newspaper reviews read, "this soloist is not worth reviewing, after all the suffering brought upon us by the Jews." The Germans did allow a temporary Jewish theater, so I became involved in performing with famous German Jewish refugee artists for the Jewish population.

Meanwhile, the Nazis brought to another theater on the next block, Jews that they had rounded up for deportations to the infamous concentration camps. Because of my involvement with the Jewish Council, who sponsored our work in the theater, we were allowed to minister to the thousands of deportees and were guaranteed we would be the last ones to go. The 'deportation theater' was a madhouse of anguish and filth, housing up to 9,000 people in a place built to seat 1,000. Sick people, old and young, crying children, were huddled together in fear of death, sleeping on louse-infested mattresses all over the floor. There were only two toilet facilities. I contracted lice and scabies all over my body, so much so, that when an opportunity did present itself for me to go into hiding, I couldn't because of my condition.

While at the theater I became good friends with Henny. Her husband had been arrested by the Gestapo, and we decided that I would stay in her house and help with her two small children. My former boyfriend, unbeknownst to me, had become a Gestapo agent out of anger against my parents. Not only did he try to destroy the Jewish people, but he sent the stormtroopers after me at Henny's place. They came at night, fired shots through the house, but failed to find us: we hid in a heavy steel dumbwaiter. The stormtroopers left, planning to return in the morning. This gave us a couple of hours to escape over the roofs of our four story house and neighboring buildings, fleeing for our lives in the dark of night.

Four Long Years, Day to Day

Thus we entered an unknown world of hiding and escape, fear and agony. For the next four years I lost all I had, my entire family, home and belongings, and had to run from death and destruction, never knowing what the next day would bring, whether I would live or die. We hid out in many places, towns and cities, and each time our arrest seemed inevitable God seemed to put a hedge of angels around us. The longest time in one hideout was 212 days in one room: never going out except by crawling over the ground in the dark to be with my parents. They were hiding in the next house until they were betrayed by the woman who was hiding us—for 25 guilders each. That was the price the Nazis paid for information about Jews in hiding or Anti-Germans listening to English radio broadcasts about the progress of the Allied forces. Alas, nothing had changed since Judas Iscariot! I saw my dear parents rounded up and taken away with bayonets at their backs. They and my lovely younger brother, Eddie, who was betrayed some time later, were all murdered in concentration camps. The only thing Eddie had taken with him was his violin, which he played professionally. He was forced to play it while our people were being tormented and gassed. After the war I met a doctor who had survived, and told me about how the Germans kept Eddie without any medication as he suffered from typhoid and got to the point where his body could no longer cope with starvation. May God help them! It takes the love of Jesus to enable us to overcome and to want to forgive; to say "Father forgive them, for they know not what they do." We forgive, He heals the wounds, but the scars remain. Space doesn't afford here for all that happened. But I can say that our God was in complete control and saw me through. Even when I was held prisoner, having been arrested with a bayonet in my own back, God was there. He freed me right out of the "lion's den," forcing them to let me go in a most miraculous way!

From Darkness to Light!

When it seemed to us that our trials would never finish, finally the war came to an end. Suddenly, it seemed from all different directions people began to talk to me about Jesus. Then, I contacted a pastor who sent, believe it or not, a German lady to me. God does have a way with things! She had married an Orthodox Jewish man, become a Jewess, and lived a Jewish life for some 33 years. Her husband died suddenly leaving her brokenhearted and grieving much, but eventually she had found Jesus as her Messiah. For the next six weeks I argued with her about this Jesus, until she asked me to read Isaiah 53 and Psalm 22. Reading Isaiah 53, I did not understand a single word. Then, as promised, I started reading Psalm 22, and coming to the 16th verse where it says "they pierced my hands and my feet", I let out one big yell, "Oh my God, that is Jesus, because He was crucified!" I remembered all the Christian paintings I had seen years earlier in that church in Amsterdam, and suddenly all of it made sense. I went back to the 53rd chapter of Isaiah and now I understood each and every word. Hallelujah! The 'scales fell off my eyes' instantly, and the first thing I said was "it's like coming out of a dark hole into the light." Though I did not know it at that point, I found out later that Jesus is called "The Light of the World." As I read the Tanakh (Old Testament) all alone in a room, Yeshua revealed Himself to me: then and there I was born again. After reading the Gospels I understood even more. Since those earlier days, God has not only furthered my concert career in the "New World," but He has enabled me to become a living testimony for Yeshua ha Mashiach (Jesus the Messiah) as my personal Savior. Now, many years later, having been in Israel visiting the places where Yeshua walked and preached, the Word has become even more dear to me. Now it is no longer a dream, but my eyes have seen where He was, and how each day He is always near to us. Amen.

"In the Shadow of the Swastika," Frieda's book about her experience during WWII's Holocaust, including numerous close calls and miraculous escapes from the Nazis, has been completed. With manuscripts in English and Russian, she is presently seeking a publisher. Additionally Frieda regularly shares her story of faith at speaking engagements around the world. Frieda's story "In The Shadow of the Swastizka" is also available on audiocassette. Please contact WMM for details.

IN SEARCH OF TRUTH
David S. Taylor

I, and my family come from the Biblical tribe of Levi. Although I bear the last name of Taylor, my family name is originally Hochman. My father was born and raised an Orthodox Jew in Brooklyn, NY. As a professional musician, he played for many years with Guy Lombardo, and on the Ted Mack show. The name Taylor came about thus: in order to leave Poland and enter the Unites States, my grandfather assumed another person's identity, and chose the name 'Schneiderman.' Later my father chose the name Taylor (tailor in Yiddish is 'schneider') as a stage name, since "Sheldon Isadore Scheiderman" wasn't exactly a 'great stage name' for a performer! Then, along came me.

I was raised in a traditional Jewish home and attended my synagogue weekly. At a young age, I was always very moved during the synagogue services, felt a deep closeness to G-d, and desired to be a rabbi when I grew up. I excelled in my early years, a Bar Mitzvah at 13, the rabbi worked with me within the instructions given to him by my devoutly Orthodox grandfather. He must have been pleased at my ceremony as I remember lots of hugs and tears on that day. The following year I was given my first job by my rabbi. I was actually hired and paid to teach the beginner's Hebrew School class at my synagogue. Every Shabbat, I sat on the bema with my rabbi and the president of our synagogue, assisted removing and replacing the Torah scroll in the ark at the weekly readings. I continued to be very involved in my synagogue until I neared 16 years of age, at which time, I became more interested in playing guitar and hanging out with my friends. At 18 years of age I was earning a living as a guitar player in a band of 'music scholarship musicians' from a local college, and I decided music/entertainment would be my career.

During this time, my sister Debbie, who, like me, also had strong ties to our synagogue and our Jewish identity, told my family she believed in 'Jesus'. Oy! Although I no longer attended synagogue and was 'far from G-d', I was shocked. I had a deep disdain for 'Christians' and especially towards 'Jesus', and I told her to never speak to me about 'Him.'

During my early 20's, I became interested in Eastern philosophy, reading books by Carlos Casteneda, Krishnamurti and others, and also studied Korean martial arts, attaining a black belt in Tae Kwon Do. Still something was missing, and my interest in whether or not a "Supreme Being" really existed began to take hold of me. Somehow, I had the sense that a person, though sincere, could be wrong in their beliefs, and when they died end up in a place they wouldn't want to be.

One day, as I was walking on the beach, about to go surfing, I remember looking up to the sky and asking aloud, "If You are really there, please show me. The Christians say that "Jesus" is the only way, the Buddhists say "Buddha" is the enlightened one, this person says this, that person says that; how am I supposed to know? Whatever it is, I just want to know the truth because I don't want to be wrong."

My career as a musician continued, I was teaching martial arts, and at 23, I married my wife, Laurie. After year and a half I discovered that I didn't want all the responsibilities that came with marriage. I wanted out. I told Laurie that I wanted a divorce, but she was raised with strong values and didn't give in to my request. Unbeknownst to me, she began to cry out to God in prayer.

Our marriage continued to get worse, until one day I woke up and out of nowhere, this question popped into my head—"What IF "Jesus" *is* the Messiah?" As the day went on this question began to bother me to no end. As days passed, being the analytical person that I am, I began seriously considering what this meant and its ramifications. In fact, I became consumed with the prospect. I knew that if "Jesus" truly was the Messiah, then I, as a Jew, should believe in Him. If He really was the Messiah then whatever He said concerning this life, the world to come, and how to get there, had to hold the greatest weight of any words that have been spoken. But was He the Messiah, or not? I <u>needed</u> to know.

One night I began to relate to Laurie that 'Jesus' was bothering me and I began asking her questions. She suggested I speak to my sister, Debbie. The next night Debbie and I went to work out at a local health club. When I saw her I said, "Debbie, Jesus is bothering me 24 hours a day. I can't get Him out of my head!" She said to me, "David, I can prove to you that Jesus is *our* Messiah." I said to her, "if you can prove to me that 'Jesus' is our Messiah from my Hebrew Bible, then I'll do whatever it takes to believe in Him. Just don't try to show me from your 'Christian Bible.' (I had always believed the Christians had changed the words in *our* Bible. I was actually scared of the 'red letter' passages I had seen.) Debbie proceeded to show me passages of Scripture from my Hebrew Bible. I was astounded!

I finished my workout and went to sit in the sauna. As I sat there, I reasoned to myself, "On one hand, if I put my trust in "Jesus", I stand to lose my family and friends, but, on the other hand, it was clear to me, from my own Hebrew Bible, that He has to be the Jewish Messiah. At that moment I opted for Messiah, and as I sat alone in a sauna at a martial arts center at 2 a.m., I confessed to G-d that I had gone my own way and not His, that I had sinned against Him, and I asked "Jesus" to come into my life. I told him that I believed He was my Messiah and that He rose from the dead on the third day.

Afterward I saw Debbie and said, "Well, I did it. This doesn't mean I have to start telling everyone about "Jesus" and go to a church, does it?" She laughed.

The next day, I told Laurie what I had done. Later that week, Laurie also prayed and placed her faith in Messiah. As that week progressed, my life became radically different. Suddenly I saw Laurie in a way I had never experienced before—I had such a love for her. It was as though I was seeing her through someone else's eyes. As I write this, we have been married for going on 25 years. This has been wonderful G-d's work in our lives. We have also been blessed with two wonderful children, Julie and Daniel, who have become Bar and Bat Mitzvah, and are also Jewish believers in Messiah with a strong sense of Jewish identity. We've been members of a Messianic Jewish congregation for 20 years, and the musical talent G-d gave me I've been privileged to use over the years as a worship leader. My love for Yeshua, and for my heritage as a Jew, is passionate.

G-d answered the prayer I prayed on the beach over 20 years ago, for Him to show me the truth. I discovered that Truth is a Person, as Yeshua stated about Himself, *"I am the way, the truth, and the life; no man comes to the Father but by Me."* He has done a truly amazing work in my life, and for this I am eternally thankful.

I'M STILL JEWISH,
& I HAVE THE MESSIAH OF ISRAEL!
STACY CORRADO

I am Jewish and was raised in a Conservative Jewish home in the greater Washington, DC area. I went through Hebrew school and was Bat-mizvahed at the age of thirteen. Looking back now, I don't think I ever understood what it meant to have a relationship with God. I went through the motions, but never really understood why.

Fast-forward fifteen years where I now live: the "Bible Belt" of Charlotte, NC where most of my friends seem to be Christians (or at least Gentile). My two best friends, who are Christians, never really talked to me about what it meant to be a believer, but I could see they were absolutely amazing women. I thought they represented how a "Christian" should be: caring, truthful, dependable, loyal and *not* overbearing. But for some reason I actually appreciated the absence of faith in our conversations.

Once, after a rather heated discussion with a friend regarding God, the Bible and eternal life, I decided to find out for myself what it was that I actually believed. In fact, I was so mad at her that I started reading anything I could on being Jewish. " I am not going to buy into this 'Jesus thing,'" I thought to myself. So I bought The Idiot's Guide to the Bible and read the entire book. At that point, I started feeling like, "Well maybe this Jesus did do some pretty amazing things, if you actually believe it at all."

Then a friend invited me to her church where, as she explained, a Jewish man would be speaking. I accepted the invitation, and to my surprise, it was awesome. There was an amazing atmosphere of love and joy as I saw Jews and Gentiles worshiping the same God together. The speaker said that even if you believe in Yeshua, you are still Jewish. Well, this was a concept that I had never even considered. It reminded me of being able to get a ticket at the amusement park for that exciting ride I always thought I was too short for.

After the service I told my two friends how interested I was in learning more. Though they did not show it, they were really excited. They later told me of all their prayers for me, and that they had been praying for me " behind my back." I now thank God for them!

A few weeks later my friend took me to *Hope of Israel Congregation.* I found the service interesting and with Passover coming up I decided to celebrate with my family. I learned that Sam Nadler had written a *Messianic Passover Haggadah* that showed how Yeshua actually celebrated Passover. So I stopped by his office to get a copy to celebrate Passover that evening. Sam and I spoke briefly about what it meant to consider Yeshua as the Messiah of Israel. Miriam actually offered to meet with me the following week to go over any questions. , In my eyes, that was so generous that I eagerly accepted.

The next day was Saturday, and I decided to visit *Hope of Israel Congregation* again. What can I tell you? The Lord touched me through the service, and when Sam invited those who wanted to accept Yeshua as Messiah to pray, I prayed the 'sinners prayer.'

It was truly an overwhelming experience. (Sort of like taking a first time bungee-jump and winning the lottery all at once!) But as my head began to clear, I began to fully understand what had happened, I realized that I was still Jewish, and now I had the Messiah of Israel with me! There are no other words for it other than I was 'born again'. (see John 3:3) Since then, my life has not been the same. Thank God for friends and their 'behind the back prayers'!

A New Heart, A New Life
Gerry Lefkowitz

Though I went to synagogue growing up, I never found satisfaction and peace in religion, Jewish or otherwise. I was a 36-year-old Jewish man and my life was a complete disaster. I was now a drug addict, drowning in a sea of pornography, profanity, perversion and selfishness. My wife, daughter and I were all going in separate directions. The worst thing of all, though, was that my heart had become hardened, bitter, empty and getting worse day by day. I was incapable of giving or receiving love, and I was certain that my situation was hopeless. Little did I know that with the Lord, nothing is hopeless.

My wife, Maida, who had been a Gentile believer for three years, had been diligently praying for my salvation. Through her gentle and quiet spirit (1 Peter 3:4), and the life of another Gentile man 'provoking me to jealousy' (Rom. 11: 11), I decided to try this "religion thing." That's when I met Yeshua, the Jewish Messiah. I admitted that I was a hopeless sinner and asked Him to come into my heart. I said to the Lord, *"Yeshua, I can't help myself. I've tried almost everything except you. Everything I try seems to make it worse. Help me, Lord!"* I said to Him, *"Please do for me what You say You can do"*, and amazingly He did!

At the very moment of salvation, two amazing things happened to me. First, He removed that bitter, hardened heart of stone, replaced it with a 'heart of flesh' (Ezekiel 11:19, 36:26) delivering me from the just penalty for my sins (John 3:36). Secondly, it seemed a 'faucet' was turned on in my heart. Slowly at first, drop by drop, my empty heart began to be filled with faith, hope and love. Today, that faucet is a constant, steady stream.

Within two weeks of accepting the Lord, I was delivered from all of my 'outward sins.' That was seven years ago. My life is completely changed since I have received Yeshua. I can now freely give and receive love. I am a 'new creation' in Messiah with a heart burdened for lost souls: just as I use to be. Though I'm constantly dependent on Messiah's grace and forgiveness, I'm now a Jewish believer who lives to study His Word, to follow His will, and to testify to His love. As Yeshua provides the opportunity, I hope to study to "show myself approved" and bring the message of Messiah to our people around the world, that they might know "Shalom b' Yeshua": "Peace in Jesus", our Messiah.

Finding the Faith of Abraham
Stewart Weinisch

I was raised in a traditional Jewish home. From the time I was nine years old until I was fourteen I attended Hebrew school, which stirred a desire to know God, and the truth about Him. At my Bar Mitzvah something 'deeper' occurred to me. I remember while looking into the ark where the Torahs were kept, I sensed I was missing something. There was a lot of religion, but there didn't seem to be any real faith. As I came to this conclusion, I made a promise to God, "Someday I will find the truth about who You are, and what You would require of me." Within a few months, however, I forgot my promise to God, and began to seek after the pleasures of the world. Although I was still practicing "being Jewish," God was the furthest thing from my mind.

A couple years later through a dating relationship with a Gentile believer in Jesus, I was challenged to consider what the Bible says about God and the purpose for my life. Plus, I had just lost my job, so I had lots of time on my hands. Over that year, we spent the majority of our time together reading the Bible. However, because I grew up believing that the New Testament was cursed, we focused only on the Hebrew Scriptures—specifically the Messianic prophecies. After a year of study and considering what I had read, I decided to visit a church. The pastor preached about the faith of Abraham (Gen. 15:6) and how Abraham was the 'father' of Jews and Christians, specifically *the father of all those who believe* in Yeshua (see Romans 4:11). I thought about this "faith", something I had pondered so long ago as a child, and realized in my heart this was something I didn't have. Soon after this I took a look at the New Testament for the first time. Upon reading the very first verse, *"A record of the genealogy of Yeshua the Messiah* (Jesus Christ) *the son of David, the son of Abraham..."*, I became convinced that *if* the Jewish people were going to have a Messiah, it had to be Jesus! It was then that I prayed to receive Yeshua as my Messiah and Lord, and I placed my trust in His atonement for my sins. Shortly after this, I sensed God working in my heart, and two things became very evident to me. First, I realized it was sort of an all or nothing deal—I had to love Him with my whole heart and live my life for Him, and second, I was going to bring the Good News of Messiah to my people. Eventually, I met my wife Shoshannah, and God has blessed us with two wonderful children who love the Lord. To this day I continue to praise His Holy name for the privilege of knowing and serving Him, and for the opportunity to proclaim His name to my people.

God's Love and A Life Long Dream
Shoshannah Weinisch

I grew up in a middle-class Jewish family and by all outward appearances, my life has always been pleasant. But like many people, I found that the 'good life' was a myth. I was lonely in a family of six. My parents fought all the time, and I never remember them ever saying that they loved me. Eventually my mother left so I took the role as 'mom,' but none of us were ever close. There was a haven for me, though: my great-grandfather's house. I would spend my summers there. His whole life revolved around synagogue and God. Though he didn't speak English, and I didn't speak Yiddish, I knew he loved me, and I knew God was in his home.

After high school, I went west to 'find myself.' I launched into a successful career at a high profile job with a computer related firm in California. Still, I was very, very lonely. I felt this big empty hole in my inner being that nothing could fill. I kept trying to fill it with relationships which ended up with me hurt and depressed. I pursued spirituality, knowledge, and philosophy, filled my hours with dancing, business, choreography, but I felt like I was being swallowed alive. People who saw me thought I had it all together. I looked busy and happy and successful. But I knew better. I knew I was dying.

Then things began to change. I found a Bible that someone had left in my apartment, and began to flip through it. For the first time, out of everything I had read, this made sense. I began to do what it talked about: turning the other cheek, humbling myself, etc., instead of beating people over the head. And it worked. I couldn't believe it! When I did things the way God said to do them it worked out for my benefit. This was real. Not only that, I was finally finding peace in my life.

Then one day as I was reading the Scriptures I realized there was a struggle going on inside of me, a power struggle, if you will. Could I commit my life to Yeshua? I got down on my knees by my bed and said, "God, if this is true—if Jesus if the Messiah—you've got to prove it supernaturally. It goes against everything I have been taught, and I can't do it on my own."

Within 24 hours my prayer was answered. When I went to pay my rent my landlady invited me in and initiated a conversation about the gospel—something she had *never* done. When I left—several hours later—I bumped into my neighbor, who for the first time began to share with me her beliefs that Jesus is the Messiah. Later at work I overheard some customers talking about Jesus. I spoke with them and they put me in touch with a Jewish believer. After we met to study the Scriptures a couple of times, I knew what I wanted. I wanted to please God. I wanted to belong to Him and have a relationship with Him. And I got what I wanted, and more! All my life I had wanted a husband devoted to me, and children. God has fulfilled the longings of my heart. I am truly amazed because there was no one further from God than me. But He forgave me, loved me, saved me. He's given me a family, my husband Stewart, and my children Melissa and Jonathan, and a life filled with Himself and His love. It's a life-long dream, and I'm living it every day!

Smart, Successful, and Hopeless
Samuil Orman

I was born in Kiev, Ukraine, of the former USSR. Both my parents are from Jewish families, and used to live in Tsarist Russia, outside the city limits, in the Jewish *shtetl,* or village. My mom and dad were secular and we did not keep Jewish traditions. We lived ordinary lives, just like every one else.

Raised with atheistic worldview, I later acquired a college degree, served in the Soviet Army, eventually married, and my wife and I had two daughters. I attained success in my career and reached the limits permissible for a Jew. As I looked at myself from the outside I was proud of my success, yet at the same time when I thought that life is going great, deep in my heart I felt empty and hopeless.

Nothing helped me: not books, films, TV/ entertainment; not even spending time with friends. I now understand that at that time the Lord was beginning to work with the 'soil of my heart.' It was at this same time that I was asked to give a couple of lectures at my workplace on an atheistic subject. I agreed, but not with enthusiasm. I began to look for materials and to read books on this theme. Along with atheistic books and other material critical of the Bible, I wanted to read the Bible itself just to be accurate. In my circle of acquaintances there was a believer who brought me a Bible: it was the first Bible that I had ever had. I began to read it, but rather than being humbled by what I read, I became proud inside: I knew something that others did not know. I used this knowledge for self-satisfaction and did not connect it to the future, eternity and salvation.

One evening the phone rang, it was that believer. He invited me to the congregation. "Tomorrow Jews will preach at our meeting. Come, it will be interesting," he said. I was very surprised. "Jews preach in a church?" I thought, "How could that be?"

From the Bible I already knew that Jesus is a Jew. But being raise a Jew, I thought that Jesus was not for Jews. But I couldn't help wondering about this. The next day I seemed to be drawn and I decided to go and hear what these Jewish men had to say about Jesus. On that morning it was raining, and it was as though somebody whispered to my ear, "Where are you going? It's cold, raining, the long way to go. You are not familiar with the route. Stay at home, there is a good show on TV." But I went. That day two Messianic Jews from the U.S. preached in the congregation: Sam Nadler was one of them. They shared their testimonies, talked about Yeshua, about Bible's prophecies. I was convinced about Yeshua. God did His job. I needed Him. When they asked to raise hands up of those who wanted to pray repentance prayer, I had no doubts in my heart that I was a sinner. I repented, believed in Yeshua and was born into a new life! That happened in April, 1989. On that day many other Jews got saved. The Lord gifted all of us with eternal life.

Since then I feel joy, knowing that I'm at peace with God. I know that from eternity God had decided to sow the seed of faith in my heart. He is holding me firmly in His hand, and someday I am going to meet Him: Yeshua my Savior!

The Gift
Ella Orman

I was born in Kiev, Ukraine into a Jewish family. My parents did not raise me in a religious environment, but rather in the spirit of humanism. We did not talk about God, but we did talk about good and evil.

After completing general education I also graduated from university. Later I got married and considered myself very happy person, leading a pretty good life: loving husband, nice house, two daughters, interesting job, great friends, nothing seemed to be lacking. We owned really big book library that my husband had been collecting for many years. We loved to read and had a circle of friends that we got together with for discussions and book exchange. One day someone gave us a Bible as a gift. We were thrilled, since in our country that was a rare commodity, and it was very difficult to get one. I have to say that my husband read Bible mostly; I just could not find time to do it, yet I was very proud of the fact that we had a Bible in our home library.

One day my husband, Samuil, found out that in a congregation in Kiev, a Jewish man who believes in Yeshua would be speaking. He was very interested what he had to share and decided to visit that congregation.

That day began a new era in our lives. Samuil came back home very excited, he could not stop sharing what he heard. It had made such an impression on him that he came to believe in Yeshua.

I could not really understand what was happening, and I thought, "It's just a phase and it will pass soon." But I have to say that I saw many changes in him and his attitude. He was reading the Bible a lot and sharing with me what he was learning about the Lord.

Our interests began to differ since he came to faith in Yeshua, and that was really bothering me. One day, I decided to go with him to the congregation to see for myself what kind group that was. Shortly after my first visit, I also came to faith in One and Only Redeemer of Israel, Yeshua as my Messiah. From that time on we have studied and served the Lord together, and God has blessed our lives. A few years later we made Aliyah to the Land of our Fathers, Eretz Yisrael, where we continue to share with our people the Good News of our loving Savior, Yeshua, the Shepherd of Israel!

Must I give up being Jewish?
Sheri Whitley

I am a Jewish native of Charlotte, NC where I grew up attending one of the local synagogues. For years I prayed for God to show me how He wanted me to worship Him. I believed Jesus was a "great man," but due to the terrible condition of the world today, I couldn't believe that He as the Messiah, or any other Messiah, had come.

My curiosity about "this Jesus" mounted after spending some time with my husband's grandmother. She loved this Jesus and talked about Him like He was her best friend. She did not question my Jewish beliefs or try to 'convert' me. I developed the utmost respect for her. For five years I sought to have the kind of loving and forgiving relationship she had with God.

I searched for years but would not accept Jesus because I thought that to do so meant me rejecting being a Jew. One of my friends eventually told me about Sam and Miriam Nadler (Sam was Jewish and believed in Jesus). I thought in order to believe in this Jesus I could no longer be Jewish and threw the phone number away. To me Jews who believed in Jesus and claimed to be Jewish were hypocrites.

I was very distraught over this whole "Jesus thing," and no one was making it any better. Some Christian friends had me pray a "sinner's prayer" with them, but it meant nothing to me. They declared I was 'in Jesus' after reciting it, but I knew nothing had changed. In my mind, there was no way I could have this Jesus unless I gave something up—my Jewishness.

One night I cried out to God to send me some spiritual guidance. I specifically prayed that I did not know who to call. Then the phone rang; it was Miriam Nadler. She got my number from someone I never even met, who was told by a friend to pray for me! I took this as a direct answer to my prayer and told her I believed Jesus was my savior and I wanted to become a "Christian."

Miriam asked "what if you could receive Jesus and still be Jewish?" "Wow, I've never heard of such a thing," I thought. She invited me to a Messianic Sabbath service. Not knowing what to expect when I arrived, I was scared. But, even though they sang and prayed "in Yeshua's name," everything was "so Jewish" I felt right at home. I began to understand I did have to give up something in order to receive Yeshua, but it wasn't my Jewish identity. In order to receive the forgiveness I had sought for so long I had to give up my sins. So that evening I prayed with Sam for Yeshua to be my Messiah, and come into my heart. I am sure the reason why God led me to Sam and Miriam is this:

God wanted me to come to Him—as a Jew!

A Simple Prayer of Faith

If you have had your questions answered, and have come to see that Yeshua is the Messiah, you now have the opportunity to receive forgiveness of sin and attain a new and eternal life from God. This simple prayer will help to focus your thoughts on God and express trusting in Yeshua for salvation.

"Dear God, I'm sorry for my sins and ask for your forgiveness of all my sins through the atonement in Yeshua the Messiah. Thank you for loving me and saving me forever...in Messiah's Name. Amen"

If you *sincerely* prayed this prayer of faith, **Mazel Tov!** You are now a child of God by faith in Yeshua!

Now you have the opportunity to spiritually grow in the love and knowledge of Messiah Yeshua. There are many materials to help you spiritually grow in God's love and your understanding of Messiah, and your relationship with God. For further information please contact us at Word of Messiah Ministries.

Welcome to the family, and Shalom!

APPENDIX
IsaiaH 52:13-53:12

IsaiaH 52:13 *Behold, My servant will prosper, He will be high and lifted up and greatly exalted.*

14 *Just as many were astonished at you, My people, so His appearance was marred more than any man and His form more than the sons of men.*

15 *Thus He will sprinkle many nations, Kings will shut their mouths on account of Him; for what had not been told them they will see, and what they had not heard they will understand.*

IsaiaH 53:1 *Who has believed our report? And to whom has the arm of the LORD been revealed?*

2 *For He shall grow up before Him as a tender plant, and as a root out of dry ground. He has no form or comeliness; and when we see Him, there is no beauty that we should desire Him.*

3 *He is despised and rejected by men, a Man of sorrows and acquainted with grief. And we hid, as it were, our faces from Him; He was despised, and we did not esteem Him.*

4 *Surely He has borne our griefs and carried our sorrows; yet we esteemed Him stricken, Smitten by God, and afflicted.*

5 *But He was wounded for our transgressions, He*

was bruised for our iniquities; the chastisement for our peace was upon Him, and by His stripes we are healed.

6 *All we like sheep have gone astray; we have turned, every one, to his own way; And the LORD has laid on Him the iniquity of us all.*

7 *He was oppressed and He was afflicted, Yet He opened not His mouth; He was led as a lamb to the slaughter, And as a sheep before its shearers is silent, So He opened not His mouth.*

8 *He was taken from prison and from judgment, And who will declare His generation? For He was cut off from the land of the living; for the transgressions of My people He was stricken.*

9 *And they made His grave with the wicked -- but with the rich at His death, because He had done no violence, nor was any deceit in His mouth.*

10 *Yet it pleased the LORD to bruise Him; He has put Him to grief. When You make His soul an offering for sin, He shall see His seed, He shall prolong His days, and the pleasure of the LORD shall prosper in His hand.*

11 *He shall see the labor of His soul, and be satisfied. By His knowledge My righteous Servant shall justify many, for He shall bear their iniquities.*

12 *Therefore I will divide Him a portion with the great, and He shall divide the spoil with the strong, because He poured out His soul unto death, and He was numbered with the transgressors, and He bore the sin of many, and made intercession for the transgressors.*

Isaiah 52:13-53:12

Isaiah 52:13 הִנֵּה יַשְׂכִּיל עַבְדִּי יָרוּם וְנִשָּׂא וְגָבַהּ
מְאֹד: 14 כַּאֲשֶׁר שָׁמְמוּ עָלֶיךָ רַבִּים כֵּן־מִשְׁחַת מֵאִישׁ
מַרְאֵהוּ וְתֹאֲרוֹ מִבְּנֵי אָדָם: 15 כֵּן יַזֶּה גּוֹיִם רַבִּים
עָלָיו יִקְפְּצוּ מְלָכִים פִּיהֶם כִּי אֲשֶׁר לֹא־סֻפַּר לָהֶם
רָאוּ וַאֲשֶׁר לֹא־שָׁמְעוּ הִתְבּוֹנָנוּ:

Isaiah 53:1 מִי הֶאֱמִין לִשְׁמֻעָתֵנוּ וּזְרוֹעַ יְהוָה עַל־מִי נִגְלָתָה:
2 וַיַּעַל כַּיּוֹנֵק לְפָנָיו וְכַשֹּׁרֶשׁ מֵאֶרֶץ צִיָּה לֹא־תֹאַר לוֹ וְלֹא
הָדָר וְנִרְאֵהוּ וְלֹא־מַרְאֶה וְנֶחְמְדֵהוּ:
3 נִבְזֶה וַחֲדַל אִישִׁים אִישׁ מַכְאֹבוֹת וִידוּעַ חֹלִי וּכְמַסְתֵּר פָּנִים
מִמֶּנּוּ נִבְזֶה וְלֹא חֲשַׁבְנֻהוּ:
4 אָכֵן חֳלָיֵנוּ הוּא נָשָׂא וּמַכְאֹבֵינוּ סְבָלָם וַאֲנַחְנוּ חֲשַׁבְנֻהוּ
נָגוּעַ מֻכֵּה אֱלֹהִים וּמְעֻנֶּה:
5 וְהוּא מְחֹלָל מִפְּשָׁעֵנוּ מְדֻכָּא מֵעֲוֹנֹתֵינוּ מוּסַר שְׁלוֹמֵנוּ עָלָיו
וּבַחֲבֻרָתוֹ נִרְפָּא־לָנוּ:
6 כֻּלָּנוּ כַּצֹּאן תָּעִינוּ אִישׁ לְדַרְכּוֹ פָּנִינוּ וַיהוָה הִפְגִּיעַ בּוֹ אֵת
עֲוֹן כֻּלָּנוּ:
7 נִגַּשׂ וְהוּא נַעֲנֶה וְלֹא יִפְתַּח־פִּיו כַּשֶּׂה לַטֶּבַח יוּבָל
וּכְרָחֵל לִפְנֵי גֹזְזֶיהָ נֶאֱלָמָה וְלֹא יִפְתַּח פִּיו:
8 מֵעֹצֶר וּמִמִּשְׁפָּט לֻקָּח וְאֶת־דּוֹרוֹ מִי יְשׂוֹחֵחַ כִּי
נִגְזַר מֵאֶרֶץ חַיִּים מִפֶּשַׁע עַמִּי נֶגַע לָמוֹ:
9 וַיִּתֵּן אֶת־רְשָׁעִים קִבְרוֹ וְאֶת־עָשִׁיר בְּמֹתָיו עַל לֹא־חָמָס
עָשָׂה וְלֹא מִרְמָה בְּפִיו:
10 וַיהוָה חָפֵץ דַּכְּאוֹ הֶחֱלִי אִם־תָּשִׂים אָשָׁם נַפְשׁוֹ
יִרְאֶה זֶרַע יַאֲרִיךְ יָמִים וְחֵפֶץ יְהוָה בְּיָדוֹ יִצְלָח:
11 מֵעֲמַל נַפְשׁוֹ יִרְאֶה יִשְׂבָּע בְּדַעְתּוֹ יַצְדִּיק
צַדִּיק עַבְדִּי לָרַבִּים וַעֲוֹנֹתָם הוּא יִסְבֹּל:
12 לָכֵן אֲחַלֶּק־לוֹ בָרַבִּים וְאֶת־עֲצוּמִים יְחַלֵּק שָׁלָל
תַּחַת אֲשֶׁר הֶעֱרָה לַמָּוֶת נַפְשׁוֹ וְאֶת־פֹּשְׁעִים נִמְנָה
וְהוּא חֵטְא־רַבִּים נָשָׂא וְלַפֹּשְׁעִים יַפְגִּיעַ:

✡ PROPHECIES OF THE MESSIAH ✡

Subject	Old Covenant	New Covenant
A descendent of Abraham	Genesis 12:3	Matthew 1:1
From the tribe of Judah	Genesis 49:10	Luke 3:33
Heir of King David	Isaiah 9:7	Luke 1:32
He was to come before temple is destroyed	Malachi 3:1	Matthew 24:1
He was to be born in Bethlehem	Micah 5:2 (1)	Luke 2:4; 5-7
He was to have a Galilean ministry	Isaiah 9:1 (8:23)	Matthew 4:13-16
He was to be born of a virgin	Isaiah 7:14	Luke 1:26,27,30
He is the Son of God	Psalm 2:7, 12	Matthew 3:17
He is God in the flesh (Mighty God)	Isaiah 9:6(5); 10:21	Hebrews 1:8-12
A forerunner was to proceed Him	Malachi 3:1	Luke 7:24
He was to be initially rejected by the nation	Isaiah 53:3	John 1:11
He was to die as an atonement for our sins	Isaiah 53:6	Matthew 20:28
He would be resurrected	Psalm 16:10	Luke 24:6-7
He will one day be accepted by Israel	Zechariah 12:10	Revelation 1:7; 7:4; 14:1-4

WMM Discipleship Materials

1. **The Feasts of Israel** - Eye-opening! The meaning of Israel's Feasts in light of the New Covenant: *Passover, Shavuot, Rosh Hashana, Yom Kippur, Sukkot, Hanukkah, Purim & more!* (232 pp.)

2. **Messianic Wisdom: Practical Scriptural Answers for Your Life in Messiah** - Discover your Jewish roots, get a better grasp on Jewish issues & living out your faith in Messiah. Essential, practical, and inspiring, this book is a must for every growing disciple of Yeshua! (200 pp.)

3. **Following Yeshua: Foundational Discipleship for Messianic Believers** - Develop a solid foundation by learning basic truths needed to grow in God's love. (65 pp.)

4. **Growing in Messiah: Vital Truths for Maturing Messianic Believers** - Answers to challenging questions facing Jewish and non-Jewish believers in Yeshua. Use as follow-up to *'Following Yeshua'*. (123 pp.)

5. **Even You Can Share The Jewish Messiah!** - Share your faith with Jewish people in a sensitive, effective manner. "Do's & Don't's", history of 'the Church' & the Jews, Messianic prophecy chart. (28 pp.)

6. **The Messianic Passover Haggadah** - The perfect guide for conducting your own Passover Seder, for family or congregational use, or to simply learn more about Passover. (40 pp.)

7. **Is Jesus The Messiah? Isaiah 53** - A four message series with an in-depth look at the Scriptures, history, and ancient rabbinical comments proving conclusively that Yeshua truly is the Jewish Messiah! (Audiocassette/CD)

8. **To The Jew 1st! / The Jewish Evangelism Seminar** - God's priority of taking the Gospel to the Jewish community from Romans 1:16,17; 8:37-9:5, *and* how to witness effectively to your Jewish friends. (Audiocassette/CD)

9. **Holocaust: A Biblical Response** - Four messages including 'Yom HaShoah'/Holocaust Remembrance Service; testimony of a Holocaust survivor; 'Escape Israel's Future Holocaust'. A moving, informative, challenging message. (Audiocassette/CD)

10. **The Blessings & Prayers in Hebrew!** - Learn the historical background and how to say sacred prayers from the Jewish/Messianic Faith, in the original language! (Tape or CD w/ Book)

Thanks be to God!

...for raising up loving friends and fellow servants in Messiah to help…

✡ proof read the text of this book: my wife Miriam and my friends Pat Campbell, Marvin Francis, Gerry Lefkowitz, Chris Turner.

✡ design the cover of this book: Pat Campbell

✡ Also, thanks to those who shared their stories of faith!

Todah rabbah, chaverim!
(Thank you very much, friends!)
Sam

For more information
please call or write:

Word of Messiah Ministries
P. O. Box 79238
Charlotte, NC
28271, USA

Phone/Fax: 704-362-1927

Be sure to visit our website at…
www.WordofMessiah.org

WORD OF MESSIAH MINISTRIES

NOTES

Notes